The Road to Dignity

A CENTURY OF CONFLICT

A History of the United Brotherhood of Carpenters
and Joiners of America, AFL-CIO, 1881–1981

By Thomas R. Brooks

NEW YORK   *Atheneum*   1981

ISBN 0-689-11214-9

Typeset and printed in the United States of America

This book was typeset, printed and bound by union labor.

 13

By Thomas R. Brooks

Clint: A Biography of a Labor Intellectual, Clinton S. Golden,   1978 (Atheneum, New York)

Communications Workers of America   1977 (Mason/Charter, New York)

Walls Come Tumbling Down   1974 (Prentice-Hall, New Jersey)

Picket Lines and Bargaining Tables   1968 (Grosset & Dunlap, New York)

Toil and Trouble   1971 (Delacorte Press, New York, 1971)

To my mother and father

CONTENTS

In any human institution, a solid past is the greatest guarantee of a sound future.

M. A. Hutcheson

FOREWORD

The year 1981 is a memorable one for the American labor movement: both the United Brotherhood of Carpenters and Joiners of America and the Federation (Federation of Organized Trades and Labor Unions, the AFL and then the AFL-CIO) celebrate their centennial. Their history has been closely intertwined from the beginning. This confluence reflects the fact that in addition to founding the Brotherhood, Peter J. McGuire, along with Gompers, was the leading figure in the formation and early development of the Federation. McGuire initiated the call for the conferences of 1881 and 1886 which formed the Federation; he chaired the first Federation convention in 1886; and he was secretary-treasurer on a part-time basis and then first vice-president.

Over the years, representatives of the Brotherhood have been at the center of the leadership of the Federation and respected and influential members of its Executive Council: Peter J. McGuire, Frank Duffy, William L. Hutcheson, M.A. Hutcheson and William Sidell (to mention only officers who have completed their active service with the Brotherhood). As the largest union in the building and construction industry, the Brotherhood has always played a strategic role in the collective bargaining and labor relations of that vital sector, locally and nationally. Moreover, the Brotherhood over the years has reflected the quintessence of an international union in the American labor movement in its philosophy, methods and governance.

The Brotherhood also well demonstrates a gradual adaptation to new circumstances—technology, competition and legislative prescriptions—while being faithful to the basic principles that have been the hallmark of the American labor movement. The establishment of 3000 local unions at one time to meet the needs and opportunities of local members in different localities and markets, and then the consolidation of these locals into district councils and their merger into approximately 2000 local unions currently to conform to new conditions and costs of service, is illustrative of this dynamic response to a changing environment. The dedication to apprenticeship while incorporating extensive changes in skills, training and job requirements; the leadership in jurisdictional machinery while pressing its strategic advantages; and the expansion into related industries and activities, all reflect the same pragmatism.

The perspective of this narrative of a hundred years of the United Brotherhood of Carpenters and Joiners of America helps us to understand how this Union really works and what it truly regards as vital. It should help us to see beyond the isolated episodes, the conflicts, and the occasional public press or media accounts. There is a strong dedication of the Brotherhood and its memebers over the century which this book helps us to understand and to appreciate.

The Brotherhood was shaped by carpenters and joiners themselves. It was not formed or led by intellectuals, government officials, or corporate leaders. All its leaders were qualified journeymen. The Union is a pragmatic response to the aspirations and experience of the working carpenter.

Officers and members of the Brotherhood will want to become more familiar with its history so as better to appreciate its rich heritage, just as our citizens need to understand the history of their nation to exercise well their responsibilities. The general reader will better understand the development and vitality of our trade unions in a free enterprise society.

John T. Dunlop
Former Secretary of Labor,
Lamont University Professor
Harvard University

I

BUILDING AMERICA

From the first, carpenters were crucial to the growth and well-being of America.

Ships had to be crafted—oak for the keel, ribs, knees and pine for planking—to carry the colonists across the fierce Atlantic to the New World. Once aboard, the passengers' fate was in the hands of the captain and his crew, but it was the ship's carpenter, "Chips," and his mate who kept them afloat, seeing to it that the decks were caulked and the seams paved with pitch. Buffeted by a great storm, the Mayflower would have sunk mid-passage with all lost had not a ship's carpenter repaired a cracked beam with "a great iron scrue."

Once ashore, the colonists' first tasks utilized the skills of carpentry. As a chronicler described the Pilgrims' first Christmas at Plymouth, all able-bodied men went ashore "some to fell timber, some to saw, some to rive [split] and some to carry, so no man rested all that day." Building craftsmen, however, were in short supply in colonial America. Of the fifty men among the Mayflower's 102 passengers (37 settlers, 11 servants and five hired hands), one was a sawyer, another, a carpenter and shipwright, and yet another, John Alden, America's first romantic hero, was a cooper. Irritated by the gentlemen adventurers crowding the tiny settlement of Jamestown, Captain John Smith ordered that those who would eat must work. "When you send again," he begged Virginia's sponsors in England, "I entreat you rather send but thirty carpenters,

1

husbandmen, gardners, fishermen, blacksmiths, masons and diggers up of trees' roots, well provided, than a thousand such as we have."

The backers of Massachusetts Bay Colony took great care to recruit men with the skills necessary for carving a new society out of the wilderness. Among the craftsmen, "a carpenter . . . being desirous to transport himself" and his family, was contracted to emigrate at the Company's expense, provided that he redeem his debt by instructing "any of the company in the trade of plow wright."

Religious freedom, economic opportunity, and land, cheap land, drew men across the sea, a hazardous voyage of 60-odd days in the best of weather. Newcomers could buy, for example, land in Pennsylvania for prices ranging from £5 to £15 per one hundred acres, that is, from one to three shillings an acre at a time when carpenters were earning about three shillings a day. Land was still cheaper in the South. At the beginning of the 18th century, you could get a hundred acres in Virginia for ten shillings and for even less in the Carolinas.

Yet, for all its cheapness, the lure of the land was not strong enough to attract sufficient skilled hands to the colonies. The crossing was grim. "During the journey," music master Gottlieb Mittelberger wrote of his 15-week trip in 1750 from Rotterdam to Philadelphia, "the ship is full of pitiful signs of distress—smells, fumes, horrors, vomiting, various kinds of sea sickness, fever, dysentery, headaches, heat, constipation, boils, scurvy, cancer, mouthrot, and similar afflictions, all of them caused by the age and the highly-salted state of the food, especially of the meat, as well as by the very bad and filthy water, which brings about the miserable destruction and death of many." One ship, the *Sea Flower*, which left Belfast in 1741 with 106 passengers, arrived after 16 weeks with sixty. Six corpses had been cannibalized.

Such voyages were not lightly undertaken, even though, as is often the case in frontier societies where goods and labor were in short supply, wages were high. As Governor John Winthrop of Massachusetts Bay Company complained in 1633, "the scarcity of workers caused them to raise their wages to an excessive rate." Three years earlier, the Massachusetts General Court (the state legislature) sought to control wages, ordering that "carpenters, joyners, bricklayers, sawyers, and thatchers shall not take above 2 shillings a day, nor any man give more, under paine of 10 shillings to taker and giver." If workers had "meate and drinke" the pay was proportionately less. The attempt to regulate the wages of skilled workmen, however, soon failed. Gabriel Thomas, a Pennsylvania historian, wrote in 1698, "Poor people can here get three times the wages for their Labour they can in England." Wages in the colonies exceeded the English scale by up to 100 percent for skilled workmen and up to 50 percent for unskilled workers. Massachusetts carpenters in 1701 earned 58.4 to 61 cents a day; in 1712, 83.3 cents. After a drop by 1743 to 40 cents a day, carpenters' wages levelled out to about 67 cents a day from 1751 to 1767.

That levelling reflected changes in the colonial economy. Towns grew and seaports flourished as white pine marked for His Majesty's Navy, barrels of salted fish and furs crowded the wharves. In 1700 the colonies were outposts on the fringes of a raw continent, numbering about 250,000 in population. By 1750, there were 1,170,000 living along the Eastern seaboard, and over the next twenty years colonial population would grow to 2,148,000. Ben Franklin predicted that "in another century . . . the greatest number of Englishmen will be on this side of the water."

Indentured servants north and south were a source of cheap labor. According to Franklin, the labor of the colonies by 1759 was "performed chiefly by indentured servants brought from Great Britain, Ireland, and Germany, because the high price it bears cannot be performed in any other way." Historian Richard Hofstadter estimated, leaving out the Puritan migration of 1630–1640, that "not less than half and perhaps considerably more, of all the white immigrants to the colonies were indentured servants, redemptioners (those who sold future labor or service to pay for their passage), or convicts." Many of the indentured young men were articled to carpenters as was young Thomas Millard in October 1640:

Know all men that I, Thomas Millard, with the Consent of Henry Wolcott of Windsor unto whose custody & care at whose charge I was

Driving a peg into a ship's hull, this early American shipwright earned more than similar European workers.

*brought over out of England into New England, doe bynd myself as
an apprentise for eight yeeres to serve William Pynchon of Springfield,
his heires & assigns in all manner of lawful employment unto the full
ext of eight yeeres beginninge the 29 day of Sept 1640 & the said
William doth condition to find the said Thomas meat drinke &
clothing fitting such an apprentise & at the end of his tyme one new
sute of apparell & forty shillings in mony: subscribed this 28 October
1640.*

How the young man fared we may guess from the following
statement attached to the indenture:

*Tho Millard by his owne consent is released & discharged of Mr.
Pynchons service this 22. of May 1648 being 4 months before his tyme
comes out, in Consideration whereoff he looses the 40s in mony wch
should have bin pd him, but Mr. Pynchon giveth him one New sute
of Aparell he hath at present.*

Colonial carpenters not only worked by the day—hence
"journeyman" for a qualified mechanic—but also contracted for
the job.* The itinerant mechanic often served as both journeyman
and master, especially in the remoter regions, as in the following
contract signed in the Shenandoah Valley in 1755:

*The sd. Johnson is to build a Framed House for the sd. Patton
. . . the house to be thirty two feet long and eighteen feet wide from
the outside to outside to be eight feet from floor to floor to be covered
and weather-boarded with clapboards two Tire of joists to be laid and
the whole job to be finished in a workmanlike manner against ye first
day o July next, for which the sd. Patton is to pay the sd. Johnson
seven Pistoles and a half as soon as the work is finished and to find
him Diet and Lodging Hawling and help to Raise the Frame and
Nails for the whole Jobb To the true performance of the above
agreement—Each party do hereby bind themselves to each other in
the Penal Sum of fifteen Pistoles to be paid to the Party observing by*

---

* The Oxford English Dictionary defines journeyman as: One who, having
served his apprenticeship to a handicraft or trade, is qualified to work at it for days
wages. Journey: a day's work. Etymologist Eric Partridge derives journey as follows:
The L adj. *diurnus* has neu. *dirunum*, turned by LL into a n. meaning "a day,"
whence VL *diurnàta*, a day's work or travel, whence OF-MF *journee* (F *journée*),
whence E. journey.

The nature of the agreement between this sawyer and his youthful apprentice in the 1800's is uncertain. Perhaps it provided only food and clothing for the youth while learning the trade.

the Party failing for witness whereof both parties have hereunto set their hands and seals this 26th Feby. 1775.

Carpenters were among the first, if not the first craftsmen to organize associations or societies that were precursors of today's trade unions and trade associations. In 1724, the Carpenters' Company of the City and County of Philadelphia was founded to establish "a 'book of prices' for the valuation of carpenter's work" on equitable principles "so that the workmen should have a fair recompense for their labor and the owner receive the worth of his money." Though journeymen carpenters were active in the Company, it appears to have been, by and large, an association of master carpenters as was the Associated Housewrights of Boston, who, in the 1780s, promoted "inventions and improvements in their art."

As early as 1689, British workmen began acting in concert to secure better working conditions. Similar action came later in America, in part, because of the openness of colonial society, and, in part, because artisans, laborers, master craftsmen, merchant-capitalists and tradesmen were caught up in the ferment that ended in a complete break between the colonies and the mother country. The American journeyman could—and frequently did—expect to set up on his own within a short time of learning his trade, or, he could strike out on the expanding frontier as a builder or farmer. Such independent-minded workmen were quick to join the Sons of Liberty, pillaging the offices of Stamp agents and royal officers in Boston, New York, Philadelphia and Charlestown. Organized in the early 1700s, the Ship Carpenters and Caulkers Club of Boston played a leading role in the events that led to the American Revolution. Members of the Club, according to tradition, dressed as Indians and dumped tea into Boston Harbor on the evening of December 16, 1773. On the eve of the Revolution, the Philadelphia Carpenters' Company offered their Hall, built in 1770, to the Continental Congress and there the Declaration of Independence was signed on July 4, 1776.

Boston Tea Party

The years that followed the American Revolution were the seedtime of American trade unionism. These early efforts were almost entirely local in character and did not involve any large numbers of working men, nor did they last very long. Nevertheless, many of the mutual aids we now associate with trade unions and collective bargaining were developed in the early 1800s. The Halifax, Canada, Society of the Brotherhood of Carpenters, organized in 1798, for example, gave as a reason for banding together: "When a brother falls into misfortune or distress that we may have it in our power to interpose with effect on his behalf. . . ." When a member died, the Society paid £2 to defray funeral expenses and a sum not exceeding £5 for the relief of the wife and £3 annually to assist the family while in her state of widowhood.

Though sick, accident, funeral and death benefits were paid by these early organizations of skilled craftsmen, collective bargaining, as we now know it, did not exist. There were no employer contributions, or jointly administered funds. Benefits were paid out of monies painstakingly amassed from initiation fees and dues. Self-regulation was the key to character and to craftsmanship. As the Constitution of the Carpenters' Society of Carlyle, Pennsylvania, put it: "It shall be the duty of every member of this society to live a sober, honest and industrious life." No member of the society "shall be permitted to measure or value any work for any carpenter in Carlyle or Cumberland County who is not a regular member of this society." A list of prices covering all descriptions of carpentry work was attached to the Society's constitution.

Self-regulation soon pitted journeymen carpenters against their employers, the Master Carpenters, over wages, the "list of prices," and increasingly, over the ten-hour day.

No one negotiated. The journeymen simply met and announced their terms, as did the house carpenters of Philadelphia when they decided in 1791 that: "In future, a Day's Work, amongst us, shall be deemed to commence at six o'clock in the morning, and terminate, at six in the evening of each day." The Master Carpenters refused and the journeymen laid down their tools in what may have been the first strike in America for shorter hours. The journeymen soon sought to undercut their employers, proposing

*Despite cramped quarters and crude tools, the colonial carpenter
and cabinetmaker crafted miracles of woodwork.*

"to undertake buildings, or give designs of *any work* in the line of
our occupation, for any one who may think it advisable to give us
employment, at 25 percent *below* [my italics] the current rate
established by the Master Carpenters, and that we will give any
reasonable security for the faithful execution of the work so entrusted
to us to perform." In their newspaper notice, the journeymen
insisted that their work was "superior to that which is executed by
boys and *pretended masters.*"

The public, apparently, was not convinced and so the journeymen lost that particular battle. Significantly, the master carpenters advanced a theory of wages that would figure in the famed
cordwainers' conspiracy case in 1806. "The wages of all artificers,"
said the Master Carpenters,

> must be regulated by the number of persons wanting employment:
> high wages induce masters to increase the number of apprentices,
> and journeymen to come from other places; low wages produce the

9

contrary effect. It is not, therefore, in the power of any set of them in a free country to keep the price of labor much below, or raise it far above a certain medium for any great length of time together, although they may, by confederating together, for some time injure themselves and others of the same occupation by undertaking work at a price lower than that at which it can be reasonably performed.

The notion that "by confederating together" workmen harmed others was expanded and incorporated into law when eight Philadelphia cordwainers were found guilty of "a combination and conspiracy to raise their wages." The journeymen shoemakers had struck for a modest increase and lost, but their leaders were indicted for conspiracy. Out of the Philadelphia cordwainer case evolved a legal doctrine holding that workers acting in concert to raise wages were engaged in a criminal conspiracy under common law. As Charles O. Gregory noted in his work, *Labor and the Law*, this doctrine "served as a formal vehicle—a legal abracadabra, if you please—in the name of which English and American judges . . . made labor unionists conform to the principles of classic economics."

The doctrine of criminal conspiracy, as set down in the Philadelphia cordwainer case, acted as a check on early unionism until it was set aside in 1842 in a Massachusetts case (*Commonwealth v. Hunt*) that, as it happened, involved another generation of bootmakers.

Carpenters, however, persisted in their struggle for shorter hours. The Carpenters' Union of Boston resolved in 1825 "That from and after the 20th of March until the 1st of September, we will not labor more than ten hours per day, unless being paid extra for each and every hour . . ." Nearly six hundred carpenters went on strike, an "unlawful action" condemned by the Master Carpenters and important segments of the public. Though the Bostonian journeymen lost, they inspired other carpenters to take up the struggle. On June 18, 1827, the journeymen house carpenters of Philadelphia resolved "to refrain from all labours . . . until the business becomes regulated by corresponding committees." They also appointed a committee of twelve to negotiate "with any committee of Master Carpenters." Their employers, however, refused to negotiate, charging that the journeymen were bent on "depriving their employers of about one-fifth of their usual time." That, said the journeymen was a miscalculation. In the longest day, they explained in an address to citizens published in the *Democratic Press*, "are but 15 hours sun, and deducting 2 hours for meals, leaves 13 hours for work; in the shortest day [of summer] there is but 9 hours sun, and of course 8 hours work averaging 10½ throughout the year, now we propose to work 10 hours during the summer and as long as we can see in the winter, taking only one hour for dinner, and we can accomplish nearly nine hours work in this matter in the shortest day. The average is 9½ hours: thus their loss would be about one-twelfth part of the time, and we maintain not any in the work."

The Philadelphia journeymen also appealed to public sensibilities: "But, fellow citizens, are we not men as well as they, and free men, too? Do we not contribute to the welfare and protection of our country as much as they do? You know we do, and we are confident that instead of cooperating with our employers you will agree with us in the justice as well as the reasonableness of our request.

"Citizens of Philadelphia, to you we appeal; with you rests the ultimate success or failure of our cause. Will you not assist us?"

The times, however, were not propitious, and their appeal fell on deaf ears. Still, their agitation drew in other workers, notably, the painters, glaziers and brick layers. As a result, it gave birth to the first effective city central labor organization, the Mechanics' Union of Trade Associations, and out of this grew the first labor party in the world, the Working Men's Party.

The rise of workingmen's parties during the years 1828–1830 in Philadelphia, Boston and New York—and ultimately of statewide movements in each of those key states—developed out of needs that then could not be met by trade unions seeking better wages and working conditions. Carpenters and other journeymen, factory workers, farmers and other workers rallied behind party platforms espousing the abolition of imprisonment for debt, universal free education, a mechanics lien law (making wages the employer's first obligation in bankruptcy), the abolition of child labor, credit,

11

currency and land reforms. The workingmen's "ticket" for the 1829 state assembly elections in New York consisted of two machinists, two carpenters, one printer, one brass-founder, one whitesmith, one cooper, one painter, one grocer, and one physician. Ebenezer Ford, a New York City carpenter, was the only one elected. But workers had better luck with their legislative proposals, which were enacted in one form or another over the next decade or so in most states.

As the workingmen's parties died out, city federations, or craft councils, began to flourish. Groups in various cities began to correspond with one another and out of these exchanges came the first national trade union federation, the National Trades' Union, formed in 1834. Before it expired in 1837, a victim of the panic and depression that followed; it sparked a renewal of the ten-hour-day struggle. Seth Luther, a Boston housewright, urged the undertaking at the NTU's second convention. He belonged to the House Carpenters' Union of Boston and had played a leading part in the ten-hour movement for carpenters, shipwrights and caulkers in the area. He travelled the New England states agitating for the ten-hour day, the establishment of free schools and the organization of the workers then being drawn to the new factories and mills springing up throughout the region.

Carpenters were organizing for the ten-hour day. As the National Trades Union *Journal* reported in May, 1835, of the Journeymen Carpenters' Society of Poughkeepsie, New York, "Perhaps a leading cause for their formation at this time was a resolution on their part to adopt the ten hour system, which is now generally prevailing." Further north, the Ship Carpenters of Whitehall, New York, organized for the same purpose, as did carpenters in Connecticut, and Indianapolis. In the spring of 1835, the Philadelphia building trades struck for the ten-hour day, establishing a work-day that lasted until the 1890s. In November 1835, the carpenters of Philadelphia announced that since "necessary expenses and expenditures" were on the rise, they would demand an increase of 25 cents on their daily wages during the summer months and of 12½ cents during the winter months. They were receiving $1.25 and $1.12½, respectively, and they set March 20 as the date for the new scale to go into effect.

Greatly encouraged by these developments, the Philadelphia Journeymen House Carpenters' Association called for a carpenters' ten-hour national convention, which was held in the City of Brotherly Love in October, 1836.

Nothing much, apparently, came of that "ten-hour convention," but as more and more Carpenters' local unions were organized around the country, an attempt to form a national union was made in 1854. Again, nothing much developed, not even a convention so far as we know. The Ship Carpenters and Caulkers, however, did succeed in organizing an international union in 1860, on the eve of the Civil War. Local unions were chartered in Buffalo, New York, Chicago, Illinois, Detroit, Michigan, Carondelet, Missouri, New Albany, Indiana, Cincinnati, Ohio, St. Louis, Missouri, and in Cleveland, Ohio. But for reasons that are not clear, Ship Carpenters' unions in Boston, New York, Philadelphia and elsewhere on the East Coast did not affiliate. The union did not last much beyond its sixth annual convention in 1866.

Still, there was continuity. John Keyes, in 1926 one of the older members of the United Brotherhood of Carpenters and Joiners of America, recalled that his uncle and grandfather were members of the Ship Carpenters' Union of Whitehall, New York, founded in 1836. In 1853, the ship caulkers of San Francisco organized to win a nine-hour day. In 1865, the local won the eight-hour day. A few years later, it was reorganized as the Journeymen Shipwrights' Association of San Francisco, and remained in existence until 1913 when it became Local 554 of the United Brotherhood of Carpenters and Joiners of America.

Gabriel Edmonston, the Brotherhood's first General President, recalled a strike parade of Washington, D. C. carpenters, successfully marching for the ten-hour day in 1849. "Son" Burke, a journeyman, carrying a large broad-axe over his shoulder, led the procession (accompanied by fife and drum), which grew in number as it passed job or shop. The following year, New York City carpenters established a daily scale of $1.75, but apathy and listlessness enabled employers to cut wages to $1.62½ a day soon after. President M. Harris of Pioneer Temple No. 1, House Carpenters' Protective Association, advocated "co-operative shops" to counter the wage cut. The New Yorkers also debated the introduction of the eight-hour day. But the Association's scale committee carried the day; urging against recourse to strikes, it suggested that 1500 men be enrolled and pledged not to work for less than $1.87½ per day from the 10th of March to the 10th of November.

Edmonston reported that the "satisfied" Washington journeymen "failed to see any use for an organization that called for the payment of regular dues. Several benevolent orders, the Odd Fellows, the Red Men, and others attracted the more provident and influential among them where the payments of sick and death benefits were the inducement . . ."

Edmonston, a native Washingtonian, born on March 29, 1839, served as an ensign of the Forty-First Virginia Infantry, Mahone's Brigade, Army of Northern Virginia (Confederate). He was wounded at Sharpsburg, and returned to his native city and his trade at the end of the war. He had fond memories of those pre-Civil War days when he served his apprenticeship. On summer Saturdays, his day ended at four o'clock, which, he later wrote, "gave me opportunity to go to the Marine Band concerts in the white house [sic] grounds, where all the pretty girls usually paraded." The apprentice's first introduction to the trade was the handle of a grindstone, "hades in a big shop on a hot day. A dull broad-axe or hatchet would take all the trade enthusiasm out of him in an hour or two." Sash, doors, blinds, mouldings and flooring were made by hand from the rough lumber. "Some of the moulding planes required two to work them," Edmonston remembered, "one to push, the other to pull. Usually the 'prentice did the pull end with a backward step." The only wood-working machinery then in use was the mortice machine invented by William Wood of Washington, D. C., worked by foot-power.

Lumber was cheap, according to Edmonston's recollections, and any thrifty man could own his own home if he wanted one. Most lumber was pit or whipsawed. "The log would be rolled over a pit on skids and one man on top would saw to the line, while the lower man in the pit only pulled down the double end and double-handed saw. The top sawyer was the mechanic and the pit man merely a cipher." Since most logs were "raft logs," boards often had auger holes in them where they had been pinned to form the raft.

Meats, vegetables, butter and eggs were plentiful and very cheap, according to Edmonston, "pork 4 to 9 cents, beef 6 to 8 cents, butter from 12 to 15 cents, and other things in proportion." (A carpenter earned 12½ cents an hour, $1.25 for a ten-hour day, or $7.50 a week.) "Good board could be had for $2 to $3 per week, including room. A city lot could be bought for $20 and up."

"The artistic temperament crops out in all trades," Edmonston once wrote, "but in none is the individual opportunity greater than in carpentry. Poor workmanship on good material apart from economic waste is a sin." For all his high regard for the old-time craftsmen and warm recollections of old times, he recognized that in the decade before the Civil War there had grown up many abuses that had a tendency to humiliate both bosses and journeymen. Piecework, he remarked, "was originally a help for the journeyman as it gave him employment at a time when he needed it most. It afterward became a menace to his livelihood when unscrupulous bosses cut the prices to the bone in order to gain an advantage over their competitors. Instead of being a winter job, piece work became the rule on a certain class of work the year around."

Other demoralizing influences developed in the decade before the Civil War:

> The lack of a decent lien law was an incentive to the dishonest contractor to adopt sharp practices. The poor journeyman was his chief victim, with the material man a close second. The scarcity of real money, the use of a depreciated currency and store orders as a medium of exchange were demoralizing. As regard liquor, the temptation to dissipation was accentuated by the fact that whiskey was only three cents a pint, while a cheaper grade could be had for twenty cents a gallon.

The Civil War added to the disruption of the old ways. As Edmonston pointed out, the call for volunteers so depleted the ranks of skilled labor that wages took a sharp upward turn and more than doubled. But at the close of the war the return of the soldiers to the trades caused the labor supply to exceed the demand and wages suffered a relapse to former conditions.

The abuses and demoralization cited by Edmonston intensified in the decades that followed the close of the Civil War. Soon those who had scorned organization would turn to brotherhood as a way out of what Edmonston characterized as anarchy. In this was the beginning of unionization for carpenters.

II

"WE WISH THE
WORLD TO KNOW . . ."

"If the strong combine, why should not the weak?"

When Peter J. McGuire posed this question in the first issue of *The Carpenter*, May, 1881, the Panic of 1873 and the six years of depression that followed were still fresh in the memories of many of his fellow craftsmen.

Wages were so far below the cost of a decent living, Gabriel Edmonston, the Brotherhood's first General President, later recalled, that the most skillful carpenters were often reduced to the point of beggary. Wages in the building trades had plummeted from a post-Civil War peak in 1872 by 25 percent or more. Hours were long; work, scarce. The introduction of piecework and machined ready-to-install building supplies made further inroads, in Edmonston's graphic phrase, "slowly but surely sapping the manhood of our craft."

True, as *The Carpenter* remarked in December 1884, "No carpenter in a city now thinks of lugging about a 300-pound chest of tools, consisting only of moulding, sash and matching planes as many . . . did in former years" in addition to the ordinary chest of tools. But a compound carver turning out six wood duplicates replaced three-score carpenters. New planing machines required only an hour and 23 minutes to dress, tongue-and-groove and bead 1,000 feet of white oak flooring. With hand planes this work entailed 110 hours. Ready-to-install parts—machine-made doors and sash, mouldings and window frames—resulted in, as McGuire pointed out, protracted periods of idleness and unsteady work. In addition, McGuire also noted:

> . . .the time-honored custom of day-work was rapidly giving way to piecework, with the minutest sub-divisions of the trade into petty branches, lessening the demand for skilled mechanics, and making the introduction of unskilled labor not only a possibility, but more and more generally the rule. The entire absence of any apprentice system . . . contributed to augment the evils. And so in this way, year by year, the once-honored craft of carpentry had been reduced from its former exalted position among mechanical callings.

As one carpenter complained in 1876, he had to become a floor-layer at 25 cents for each "square" laid, able to lay only three hundred square feet a day.

Even the return of prosperity in 1880 failed to benefit the carpenter. As Edmonston noted, the hours of a day's work and the changes of season served to undercut the carpenter's position. "In the fall of 1880," he wrote, "when wages were nominally $2 a day [in Washington, D.C.] the journeyman was required to work 'three-quarter time' by reason of the shortening of the hours of daylight, hence his wages were reduced to $1.50 for one day's labor. Piece work . . . netted him less than $1 for his day's work." McGuire pointed out that a kit of tools cost from $30 to $150. Carpenters, he added, must live 365 days on nine months' work, risk accidents, exposure to all weather, undertake a long apprenticeship. "Men in dry goods stores who work 308 days in the year at $10 a week, earn as much as a carpenter at $2.25 a day."

Carpenters all around the country drew from the above conditions the lesson spelled out by McGuire in the first issue of *The Carpenter*:

> In the present age there is no hope for workingmen outside of organization. Without a trade union, the workman meets the employer at a great disadvantage. The capitalist has the advantage of past accumulation; the laborer, unassisted by combination, has not. Knowing this, the capitalist can wait, while his men, without funds, have no other alternative but to submit. But with organization

the case is altered; and the more wide-spread the organization, the better. Then the workman is able to meet the employer on equal terms. No longer helpless and without resources, he has not only his union treasury, but the moneys of sister unions to support him in his ventures.

Carpenter unions were organized, or reorganized, in scores of cities around the country with the return to prosperity in the late 1870s and early 1880s. There began what the old timers called "a movement" for higher wages. As "Trade Reports" in the first issue of *The Carpenter* indicated, these were mostly successful. From New Haven, Connecticut, union men reported wages from $1.75 to $2.25 a day and that their union would strike for $2.50. Carpenters in nearby Bridgeport wrote that the trade was "extremely busy; $2.75 to $3 per day; prospects of advance. *Union organized.*" (Italics added.) So it went across the country with union wages ranging from $2.25 to $3.25 a day; up 25 cents a day wherever the union locals were active and strong. But San Francisco ominously reported: "Trade improving: $2 to $2.75. Continual flux of men keeps wages low."

It was this "continual flux" that triggered the organization of a national union. But the catalyst, the prime mover, was an ebullient, red-headed joiner with a rich baritone, Peter J. McGuire.

Born on July 6, 1852 of Irish immigrant parents, young Peter left school at eleven to hawk papers in the streets, black boots, hold horses for gentlemen riders, run errands and sweep out shops to help support his mother and three sisters while his father fought for the Union and to free the slaves. Evenings, he studied ancient philosophers, delved into economics, history and political theory at Cooper Union, the celebrated academy for the poor, founded by philanthropist Peter Cooper in 1859. At 17, Peter became an apprentice joiner at Haynes Piano Company and a member of the Cabinet Makers Union of New York.

While at Cooper Union, young McGuire joined a debating society where he first met Sam Gompers, who described him as "a fiery orator with a big heart." The two became life-long friends despite a profound difference in temperament. When club-swinging police broke up the Tompkins Square unemployment demonstra-

Peter J. McGuire

tion, which McGuire and Gompers had helped to organize, McGuire intensified his agitation on behalf of the socialist cause while Gompers became convinced of the futility of political radicalism. A natural-born joiner and organizer, McGuire was a founder of the Social Democratic Party of North America. He was an indefatigable speaker, making, for example, 107 speeches on a six-week tour of the South, Middle West, and the East, riding the rods most of the way, walking the rest. He once walked from Salem to New Bedford to agitate for strikers at the Wamsutta Knitting Mills. In 1878, he campaigned for the Greenbackers, and in October of 1878 moved to St. Louis, where he went to work in a furniture factory without, however, ceasing his efforts on behalf of his fellow workmen. In 1880, he secured the passage of important labor bills in the Missouri state legislature and was instrumental in organizing the Labor Bureau of that state.

Increasingly, however, the twenty-eight-year-old McGuire devoted more of his time and talents to the cause of his fellow carpenters. R. M. Sender of Santa Barbara Local 1062 described the McGuire he knew when a lad in St. Louis as a red head, wearing what he called a "Connecticut" straw hat. He was a fluent and forceful speaker, a commanding figure on soap-box or public platform. A well-built man, fairly tall with a mustache and fiery blue eyes, McGuire seemed to possess an inexhaustible store of energy. While enroute to the West, a young Irish immigrant, Patrick Henry "Pinhead" McCarthy, later an important figure in the Brotherhood and Mayor of San Francisco, met McGuire. He described him as having a great advantage for union work in St. Louis because he could speak German fluently. (Many of the carpenters there at the time were German immigrants or of German extraction.) McCarthy reports McGuire as working on a job known as Filley's Foundry when carpenter unionism caught on. "Exposed as I am all day to the biting cold is pretty hard on me," McGuire described his work that winter of 1881. "We work 120 feet from the ground, are pretty well exposed building a self-supporting roof. The arctic weather lately kept us idle for several days, but I keep the job because it will last until summer and it pays $2.50 per day of nine hours."

While working on his wintry job, McGuire found time to help fellow carpenters, German-American socialists Gustav Luebkert and August Oberbeck nurture the three branches of the St. Louis carpenters' union. Oberbeck became the editor of the German language section of *The Carpenter*. On March 17, 1881, McGuire and his associates called a mass meeting at a place called Euricks Cave, located at Washington and Jefferson Avenues, in support of a wage increase proposed for the 1st of April. Though the speeches were characterized by moderation of language and earnestness of expression, the carpenters resolved to strike if their demands were not met.

McGuire presided over eleventh-hour negotiations to forestall a strike; these successfully concluded agreements with 112 firms on a rate of $3.00 a day. (Before the union, carpenters had been working ten to sixteen hours a day for $1.25 to $2 a day, and very few at the latter price. In 1880, the union established a $2.50 rate.) On the south side of St. Louis, however, where the union was weakest, a strike ensued, supported by a 25-cent assessment levied on the victorious carpenters. The St. Louis carpenters asked "all carpenters to steer clear until our troubles are fully settled." They announced plans for an intelligence office or labor bureau so that "strangers" might be provided jobs at union scale. "We also take care of our sick and disabled members," they announced, "and help each other procure employement. *Union has done so much for us that we wish the world to know it.*" (Italics added.)

But the St. Louis carpenters discovered, as they later reported to the first Carpenters' convention, that their advance in wages would soon be lost through the influx of men from other cities where wages were lower. Day after day men came from other States where wages were $1.75 to $2.

Then it was that they concluded the only resort was to form a National Union, unite all local unions, organize the low-paid towns, and raise the wages to a general standard throughout the country.*

Typically, McGuire, after the $3 victory, had plunged into support of a strike of St. Louis street-railway workers. Still, he found time to publish *The Carpenter* and to open correspondence with carpenter groups throughout the country. McGuire sent out some

---

* The census of 1880 gives a total of 373,143 carpenters in the United States. About 100,000 of these were foreign born, 30,000 in Germany and about 15,000 alike in Great Britain and in Ireland.

500 letters in the spring of 1881; about one-half replied to his overtures. In all, sixty-two unions with a membership of 18,000 pledged support to the idea of a national union. A convention was called to meet in Chicago on August 8, 1881. †

The Chicago carpenters offered to house and feed delegates. "The big pot and the little pot were put on the fire," Edmonston later recalled, "the best blue-edged plates and the newest table linens were brought into use. The good wife worked extra hours without additional pay to contribute her share toward the success of the enterprise."

Edmonston and his fellow D.C. delegate, Dave Cregg, rode twenty-six hours in the day coach to save their local union the expense of sleeping-car fare. The round-trip coach tickets cost nine dollars each, three times the District's highest daily rate. After scrubbing their faces to get rid of soft coal soot and grit, they plunged into the business of the convention. The delegates met in the spacious Trades Assembly Hall, artistically draped with flags and banners and suitable emblems. A model of the Dresden cathedral steeple and of a spiral staircase ornamented the front of the stage and attracted high encomiums for its excellent workmanship.

There were, of course, differences as to how best to proceed with the building of a national union. According to Edmonston, the convention was divided into two factions, one wanting a strictly protective Union and the other, a benevolent body, leaving the protective features to the locals. * The Chicago Tribune reported a division over representation for German-speaking carpenters and one between socialists and anti-socialists. The delegates authorized

---

† Thirty-six delegates were present, representing eleven cities—St. Louis, Chicago, Cincinnati, Indianapolis, Philadelphia, Buffalo, New York, Washington, D.C., Detroit, Cleveland and Kansas City—and 12 local unions with a total of 2,042 members.

* The "benevolents" desired a national union with the sole function of providing benefits, chiefly death and disability benefits. The "protectives," though not opposed to benefits, wanted a national organization that would strengthen local unions "movements," efforts including strikes, to regulate working conditions, gain shorter hours and better wages.

the publication of *The Carpenter*, half in English and half in German. The German pages—and later a French page provided for French-Canadians active in New England—were an important feature of the publication for decades. The convention almost became a cropper when the Cincinnati delegation walked out and the remaining anti-socialists insisted on an apology to J. R. Smith, a Cincinnati delegate who shared an evening rally platform with McGuire and had the temerity to declare that while he was not afraid of the word "strike," he did not agree with those of his fellow craftsmen who denounced the capitalist. McGuire and Edmonston patched up a compromise that saved the convention and launched the union. In the years ahead, the union would develop both its "benevolent," i.e., benefit features and its "protective" capacity. Initially, however, as Edmonston later wrote, it seems to have been a desire of the majority to build a cheap National Union so that it might not bear too heavily on the locals.

Nonetheless, the first convention established one full-time officer, the General Secretary, to be paid $15 a week out of a 5¢ monthly per capita,† set dues of not less than 25 cents a month, initiation fees of not less than $2, inaugurated a national working-card system, prohibited piecework and established a strike "assistance fund" financed by a ten-percent tax on each local's income. Strikes were to be sanctioned by the executive board, which then would authorize a strike benefit of $4 a week per member to commence after two weeks. The General Secretary was instructed to enter into relations with the carpenters of Canada with a view to bring them within the fold.

† *The Carpenter* carried advertisements to cover costs of publication: any deficits were met out of the 5¢ per capita, which also had to cover the costs of benevolent features adopted at the Second Convention in 1882. On the death of a member six months in good standing, his heirs or family were entitled to $240. In case of the permanent disability of a member by an accident occurring to him while working at the trade, he was entitled to $250 on two years' membership, and $100 on 6 months' membership. Should the wife of a married member die, he received a $50 funeral benefit. In addition, there was a modest per capita to the newly established Federation of Trades. As Edmonston wryly put it, "If any trade unionist can point out where so cheap a National Union ever lived longer than a single month I would be glad to know the fact."

The Brotherhood of Carpenters and Joiners of America, the name then adopted, was to be a union broad enough to embrace every carpenter and joiner in the land. The concerns of the founders were reflected in the resolutions adopted. The delegates believed that "the best interests of our trade demand shorter hours of labor, in order that labor-saving machinery may not be so extensively employed in reducing the compensation due to skilled labor." They wanted no distinction drawn "between work in winter and summer, to the loss of wages in the former season, as the physical danger attending manual toil is greatly increased during the winter months." The resolution on political action, no doubt, was a compromise between the socialists, who wished endorsement of a socialist or labor party and those opposed. It called for abandoning either political party and pledged support for candidates who, they were assured, would best represent the laboring classes. The delegates wanted an end to monopolies and passage of uniform lien laws to secure the wages of labor first, and material second. First mortgages on real estate were to be granted without long stays of execution or other delays. They urged abolition of convict labor, the establishment of building trade leagues and employment bureaus to facilitate the employment of local and travelling members of the Brotherhood, and an international confederation of building trades organizations; they endorsed the newly established Federation of Organized Trades and Labor Unions. P. J. McGuire was elected General Secretary, and Gabriel Edmonston, General President of the infant Brotherhood. John D. Allen, subsequently the second General President of the organization, was elected to represent the Brotherhood at the first convention of the Federation of Trades in November 1881 in Pittsburgh. *

* Allen, incidentally, was an interesting figure. He was born in Harveysburg, Ohio, on April 27, 1850. In October, 1879, he reorganized Assembly No. 18 of the Knights of Labor of Philadelphia as a carpenters' group, later chartered as Local 8 of the Brotherhood. Allen headed the local for a number of years, leading a three-week strike in 1882 over a demand for a 50 cents-a-day increase. It ended in a compromise—25 cents. Allen then became a leading architect; designing, building and remodeling, among others, the Chestnut Street Theatre and Opera House in Philadelphia, the Fifth Avenue Theatre in New York City and the Academy of Music in Wilmington, Delaware.

GABRIEL EDMONSTON
1st *General President U.B. of C. & J. of A.*
1881

Other officers elected at the first convention were: John Ritter, New York, first vice president; W. D. Black, Chicago, second vice president; A. W. Oberbeck, St. Louis, third vice president. President Edmonston named eighteen district organizers: R. W. Comfort and J. P. Goodwin, Chicago; John Ritter and Jacob Schneider, New York; J. C. Schneider, J. M. House, Buffalo, New York; John Beasley and John E. Walton, Kansas City, Mo.; J. D. Allen and Chas. L. Dodd, Philadelphia; D. McIntosh and Jos. Buddinger, Cleveland; J. M. Kerr and I. N. Evans, Detroit; Casper Heep and Robert Stofiel, St. Louis; Edward Wayson and John Henderson, Washington, D. C.

As it turned out, Edmonston substituted for Allen at the founding convention on November 15, 1881 of the Federation of Organized Trades and Labor Unions, the precursor of the American Federation of Labor. McGuire had drafted the call to the convention, but was in Europe that fall at a meeting of socialists and trade unionists, the International Workingmen's Congress. *

The Brotherhood backed "federation" of unions at both the local and national level. The move was seen as a way of strengthening as well as building the labor movement. In Washington, D. C., as an instance, the carpenters in the spring of 1881 visited the bricklayers, granite cutters and printers' unions to urge the orga-

---

* McGuire went as a delegate from the Socialist Labor Party and he took pains to inform members of the union that this was done without any expense to the Brotherhood. Sam Gompers advised against his going "for I feared his new organization would wither in his absence. Fortunately, my fears were not realized." Edmonston recalled: "Before he left he wrote to me from St. Louis that he had employed Gustav Luebkert to perform his duty until his return, which occurred some months after. I wrote to St. Louis and became satisfied that Brother Luebkert, while unpopular because of his rampant socialism, was thoroughly honest and trustworthy and I acquiesced in his selection as Secretary pro tem. Whenever it was necessary I wrote to delinquent locals to forward their per capita to Brother Luebkert in order that *The Carpenter* should appear on time. Brother Luebkert filled his place in a satisfactory manner and edited the paper without imposing his hobby on the Brotherhood. The absence of Brother McGuire, however, made the duties of General President particularly onerous. I was obliged to work ten hours each day and had to sit up sometimes long past midnight writing answers to letters that were brought by the double handful in each mail."

nization of a central labor body, which became the Federation of
Labor of the District of Columbia. The four crafts were the only
"open" trade unions in the District at the time. The plasterers,
though organized, Edmonston once remarked, "were so secret that
they could not mention the name and expressed it by five stars,
★★★★★."

The Federation of Organized Trades was a rather loosely
organized affair with no full-time officers at the start. Edmonston
was elected to serve on its Legislative Committee, in effect the new
organization's executive body chaired by Sam Gompers. Later he
became its secretary. McGuire, on his return from Europe, drafted
a "memorial" for the Federation's second convention in Cleveland
in November, 1882:

> We favor a Federation of Trades and Labor Unions, organized as an
> industrial body, and not as a political one. Its work should be to
> bring all trades together in closer unity for the better protection of
> our interests as workmen. . . . We favor this Federation, because it
> . . . preserves the industrial autonomy and distinctive character of
> each trade and labor union. . . . It organizes [workers] in their
> respective trades unions, and makes the qualities of the man as a
> worker the only test of fitness, and sets up no political or religious
> test of membership. . . . While industry prevails, trades unions will
> exist, and this necessitates organization by trades, for the men of one
> craft will more readily unite for their collective interests as they are
> brought closer in contact with each other, and become impressed
> with the necessity of organization. . . . The principle of unionism
> . . . should be extended to effect the national and international
> organization of each trade. And it equally follows that these trades
> and labor unions should be combined in a Federation of Trades and
> Labor Unions.

McGuire spelled out the fundamentals for a successful national
trade union center. But the national unions were as yet too divided
and too weak to heed his advice. Though the Brotherhood gave
what support it could, the Federation of Organized Trades remained, in historian Philip Taft's apt phrase, "anemic and inactive."

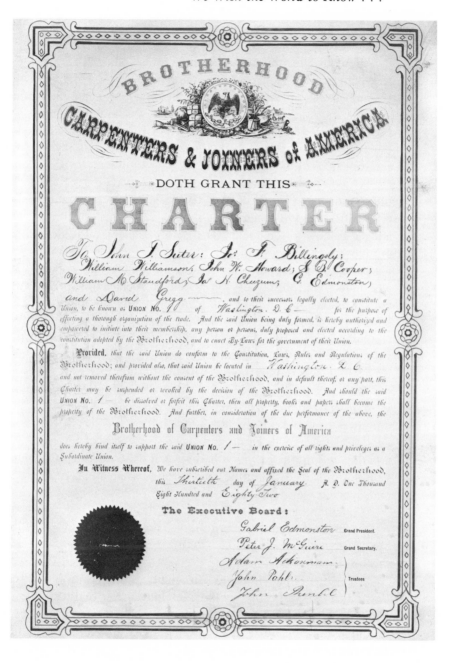

Unionists were not in a position to give life to McGuire's "memorial" until 1886.

Beset by "the ubiquitous botch with his briar-root saw, battered jack-plane and defective square," and the "Jerry" builder driving his men to scamp their work, the carpenters expressed their pride of craft in building their new union. "Without organization," McGuire stated in an early issue of *The Carpenter*, "the dignity of our trade will sink through the cupidity of unfair employers, who care but little for good workmen."

Good conduct was a matter of some importance to these trade union pioneers. One of the first rules adopted by the union barred drunks from union meetings. Drinking was dangerous on the job and destructive of character off the job. Benefits were denied on grounds of excessive drinking. For years, a regular feature of *The Carpenter* carried photographs of errant craftsmen, workers who absconded with funds or the wives of their fellows. An early constitutional amendment imposed a $5 fine on members who knowingly signed the nominating petition for an unqualified candidate. As Edmonston remarked of building the union, "If our structure is to be a grand edifice, reflecting credit on its builders, let us do our work thoroughly, using only such materials as insure durability. . . . The most important duty of each individual member is to *assert his position*, not only at his work, by studying his employer's interests justly and fairly, but by a constant course of conduct such as will command the respect both of his employer and the community in which he lives." It behooved the carpenters, Edmonston added, "to unite, and through association use our best endeavors to elevate our trade above that of mere wage-workers."

Agitation, Education and Organization were, as Edmonston once remarked, about the only stated policy of the union in the early years. There was no paid staff, except the General Secretary; the headquarters were changed every two years, from St. Louis to New York to Philadelphia to Cleveland, until it was decided to locate the national office in Philadelphia for ten years, ending in 1896. The executive board of five members was elected by the local unions within ten miles of the headquarters to facilitate meetings at a time when transportation was slow. The national officers, including a new president elected every year,* worked in their respective locales for the most part. District organizers worked when their home locals could afford to pay their salaries and expenses.

The indefatigable McGuire moved with the union, agitating, educating and organizing all the while. In New York City, on May 18, 1882, he proposed at a meeting of the New York Central Labor Union that a day be set aside annually to honor labor. The day, he suggested, should be celebrated by a street parade, which would publicly show the strength and *esprit de corps* of the trade and labor organizations. The first Monday in September, he said, would be appropriate because it would come at the most pleasant season of the year, nearly midway between the Fourth of July and Thanksgiving and would fill a wide gap in the chronology of legal holidays. Ten thousand marchers strode up Broadway from City Hall to Union Square and then assembled in Reservoir Park for a picnic on September 5, 1882.

The Federation of Trades and Labor Unions took up the holiday in 1884, and parades were held in cities throughout the northeast. Oregon became the first state to legalize Labor Day in 1887. Colorado, New Jersey, New York and Massachusetts soon followed suit. After a decade of lobbying, Rep. Amos J. Cummings (D-NY) a member of Typographical Union No. 6, introduced a bill in Congress which became law on June 28, 1894, establishing Labor Day as a national holiday.

Peter McGuire, the "Father of Labor Day" was a bachelor until the spring of 1884 when he met, wooed, and married on

---

* These were:

1st	GABRIEL EDMONSTON	1881
2nd	JOHN D. ALLEN	1882–1883
3rd	JOHN P. McGINLEY	1883–1884
4th	JOSEPH F. BILLINGSLEY	1884–1886
5th	WM. J. SHIELDS	1886–1888
6th	D. P. ROWLAND	1888–1890
7th	H. W. KLIVER	1890–1892
8th	HENRY H. TRENOR	1892–1894
9th	CHAS. B. OWENS	1894–1896
10th	HARRY LLOYD	1896–1898
11th	JOHN WILLIAMS	1898–1899

New York City—Grand demonstration of workingmen, September 5th—the procession passing the reviewing-stand at Union Square.

October 6, Christina Wolff, a young woman from Staten Island, New York. Their first child, Lillian, was born in 1886, the year the union moved to its headquarters in Philadelphia. The McGuires moved to Camden, just across the river in New Jersey, where they would live the rest of their lives.

"When we first commenced active agitation," W. F. Eberhardt, the corresponding secretary of Philadelphia Local 8, reported in the February, 1882 *Carpenter*, "we went from ward to ward in our city. We sent a circular with a ticket of admission by mail to every carpenter living in said ward. Out of every hundred so notified about six responded; if we notified 325, from 20 to 26 strangers would be present, and from 5 to 8 would join us on that evening. We did not stop or get discouraged; we went on, and it is not quite a year since we commenced this plan. We then had less than 50 members and now we have grown to great proportions. Those small meetings paid, no matter how discouraging they might have appeared to some. We are having these meetings now; every such meeting is like making a hole in a tub of water; there is a flow of candidates from that section of the city after each of these meetings. My reason for writing this is not merely to tell something, but with a view to stir up other cities. Let the active men gather themselves together and put the members of their Union to work. It elevates and improves them; they learn if they go to work. It strengthens their Union and increases their treasury."

Other local unions put on "walking delegates," in part, in response to changing conditions within the trade. As James Lynch, the first walking delegate of the New York City carpenters (appointed in July 1883), put it, "a cloud . . . threatened the stability of our union. It was the sub-letting of work, known as 'lumping.' A large number of brown-stone fronts were being built by speculators. They would build a block seven hundred feet long and four or five stories high; letting out such work as setting door frames to one class of men at so much each; the putting on of casings to another. This led to special classes of workers known as 'door-hangers,' etc., according to their special work." This was opposed by the union but it was unable to stop the practice, so Lyons was appointed a walking delegate to keep after the Lumpers.

33

Volunteer organizers spread the gospel. C. C. Crossley, of Struthers, Ohio, Local Union No. 171, many years later recalled how he got "on the job" by offering for sale the Fales Bench Plane:

> I spent six months of my life and paid my own expenses and worked every town on both sides of the Hudson River from Albany to New York City, and went on East through the New England States to Bangor, Me., taking in every town and hamlet where I could find a carpenter at work, even taking in Marthas Vineyard and Nantucket Island, . . . but as soon as the boss found I was talking unionism I had to move on.

Organization was difficult. Carpenters were plagued by the cycle of boom and bust endemic to the building industry. Local union leaders echoed Edmonston's complaint that many desired a cheap union. W. W. Weston wrote from Hamilton, Canada, in December, 1882, "Over 130 had placed their names on our list, but when it came to paying the initiation fee our number was reduced to thirteen; it has since increased to twenty-seven members." Pointedly, he added, "Some non-union members have joined the Knights of Labor because it is cheap—ten cents a month dues."* More encouraging news came from Toronto where 600 men "came out" on April 6 and soon a thousand were on strike. The Printers donated $250; the Bricklayers, $200, while the Stone Cutters and Seamen emptied their treasuries. A concert raised $400, and the strike was settled with a 25 cents-a-day raise. "Some bosses," wrote W. H. Fogwell of Toronto "used to cut wages in the winter, but that thing has played out since our union started." A year later, in May, 1883, he reported, "We find no difficulty in paying our just debts and dues, we insure each member's tools against both fire and theft, we have money in the bank and we owe no man anything except good will to all Brothers."

Success was often measured in small increments. *The Carpenter* reminded its readers each month that seven men who were house

---

* Initiation fees and dues were regulated by local unions. Some set an entrance fee at $2, others, at $5, but in no case were they allowed to be less than one dollar. Dues were 50 cents a month in most locals; none allowed less than 25 cents a month. Efforts were made from the first to establish uniform dues and uniform initiation fees, but these were unsuccessful.

carpenters and joiners, of good moral character and sound health, and who could command the average wages, could organize a local union. The June, 1882 issue found it cheering news that from seven to nine new members were added to the rolls of the Indianapolis local union at every meeting. That union was composed of many of the oldest and most respectable gentlemen comprised in the carpenters' and joiners' trade. Some locals, L. J. B. reported from Chicago in the spring of 1883, "have now a sick benefit and fifty cents dues, and I see others falling in line. [Such locals] have been successful . . . while the cheap Locals have all, or nearly all fallen behind."

Strikes were often undercut by inter- and sometimes intra-union rivalries as well as by the availability of non-union labor. In Cincinnati, the strike of 1882 was crippled by rival factions, despite a valiant effort by McGuire to secure harmony. Non-union carpenters from Covington and Newport, Kentucky, crossed the Ohio River to scab. Some officers acted treacherously by sneaking back to work after a few days. The city was full of floating carpenters. Striking "chips" in Kansas City had to contend with carpenters from Leadville, Denver and the Territories on their way back East, dead broke. After two-and-one-half weeks out, however, the Kansas City carpenters carried their demand for a $3 day on nearly three-fourths of the work in that city.

Strikes, however, were not undertaken lightly. "The most important point is the state of the trade," warned Gustav Luebkert in *The Carpenter*. "If it is slack, don't strike, but wait for a better time." McGuire drafted a strike guide. It urged that strikers appoint a strike committee, hold daily meetings, draw up a list of those on strike, and appoint pickets "at once to watch the various jobs and also the railroad depots and steamboat landings." Foremen "should quit work with you, for their interest should be with the men. If the men are advanced, they are likewise advanced." Every job ought to be picketed, but "never allow the men formerly on the job to act as pickets." Whenever a carpenter arrives from elsewhere, "take charge of him, and whenever a toolbox arrives, ferret out the owner, and . . . look after such new comers, treat them fairly and provide for them that they may not go to work against you." Men

Before the days of white overalls, carpenters were forced to wear makeshift clothing and aprons on the job. Ms. Ruth A. North of Stratford, Conn., discovered the picture above in an old family album, showing two unidentified carpenters preparing to do a days work. The picture is believed to have been taken about 1900.

should "keep away from seeing the boss of the job from which they quit." If the boss wants them, he should come to strike headquarters. "When you come out in a body, go back to work in a body." Should a boss settle, his men should be permitted to return to work. And they should contribute to the aid of those still out.

Growth in membership, at first, was slow, about a thousand new members each year until 1886, when McGuire reported a gain of 18,481 in two years, a rise to 42,521 in 214 local unions. The union's jurisdiction stretched from Union No. 83 of Halifax, Nova Scotia, to San Francisco, Los Angeles and British Columbia, with 11 local unions in Canada, and more than a score of unions in the Southern States, as far south as New Orleans and Galveston. In the Southern states, McGuire reported, "the colored men working at the trade have taken hold of the organization with avidity, and the result is that the Brotherhood embraces 14 unions of colored carpenters in the South." L. E. Rames, secretary of the colored local in Charleston, South Carolina, was elected Fourth Vice-President of the Brotherhood at the 1884 Convention in Cincinnati. When, in the company of several fellow delegates, he was refused services in a coffee house, the convention unanimously passed a special resolution: "In this indignity offered to Brother Rames . . . we recognize a gross and ignorant insult to our body worthy of the severest rebuke at our hands." The delegates called upon the citizens and working people of Cincinnati "to withdraw all patronage from the 'People's Restaurant,' and hold it up to public execration." The Brotherhood's constitution and documents were translated and printed in German, French, Bohemian and the Scandinavian languages.

Increasingly, McGuire and the Brotherhood agitated for shorter hours. "Two hours a day less," McGuire preached, "means that five men have to be hired in place of four to do the same amount of work, and thus men now idle would be able to live." But the eight-hour day was a moral question as well as an economic one for McGuire and his followers. "This labor agitation," he told a Faneuil Hall audience, principally of carpenters from the Boston area, in March of 1886, "is not, as some imagine, the rantings of a howling mob, nor is it simply a struggle to get possession of more

37

grub. . . . It is a struggle to secure an opportunity for physical, mental and moral improvement among the people, and the 8-hour movement is the entering wedge."

"While men are poorly paid and working long hours for a bare existence," McGuire constantly reminded his audiences, "there cannot be that progress necessary for the perpetuity of good government and the welfare of man." Eight hours' work, he added, "would give more leisure to all employed. They will read and their wants will increase. They will want carpets on their floors and pictures on their walls. They will reach a higher civilization. . . ."

That was the mission of the Brotherhood in the struggle that lay ahead for shorter hours.

III

"WE HAVE
SPREAD THE GOSPEL . . ."

The struggle for the eight-hour day proved to be the making of the Brotherhood—and of the American Federation of Labor.

Agitation for shorter hours has a long history in this country, much of it carried on by carpenters. One of the earliest strikes for shorter hours was that of Philadelphia carpenters who demanded a ten-hour day in 1791. The standard ten-hour work day, however, was not achieved until the mid-1830s, when the Philadelphia building trades once again struck for the ten-hour day. Skilled tradesmen elsewhere soon achieved the ten-hour goal. In 1840, President Martin Van Buren, a New Yorker who owed much to the support of workingmen, issued on March 31 an executive order establishing the ten-hour day on all government works.

Edmonston attributed the origins of the eight-hour agitation to the Masonic fraternity. "It was in the latter body," he wrote in the March, 1903 issue of *The Carpenter*, "that I received my first inspiration as to its justice and value."* The first to attain the eight-

* The role of the Masons in the early development of trades unions has been underplayed by most historians. Uriah Stephens, a founder of the Knights of Labor, was a member, as were a number of other early leaders of labor. Edmonston belonged; so did most if not all the General Presidents of the Brotherhood. The influence of the Order is apparent in the Brotherhood's ritual, and in its logo with the square and compass and slogan, *Labor Omnia Vincit*. Sam Gompers was once warned by a mine guard, a fellow Mason, that his company was having him watched. He wrote in his autobiography, "I have frequently found that my affiliation to the Masonic order has been a protection to me."

hour day may have been the Granite Cutters of Columbia, South Carolina, who did so, according to Edmonston, prior to 1861. Ira Steward, a self-educated Boston machinist, gave it further impetus with his "Eight Hour Leagues," which agitated for the legal establishment of the eight-hour day shortly after the Civil War. The leagues sought pledges from candidates for public office, opposing those who would not sign. Carpenters were active in the leagues; C. W. Gibson, a Brotherhood General Executive Board member in the 1890s, organized the Eight Hour League in Norwich, Connecticut in 1866. He also became National Secretary of the National Labor Union, which was instrumental in promoting Eight Hour Leagues around the country. Congress adopted the eight-hour day for federal employees in 1869. Illinois, Wisconsin, Connecticut, Missouri and New York passed state laws, but allowed employers an escape, a right-to-work loophole that permitted labor contracts requiring ten hours a day or more.

The Baltimore carpenters won the eight-hour day in 1865. Peter W. Birk, a Second General Vice President of the Brotherhood, who was born in Copenhagen in 1832, came to the United States as a child, served three years during the Civil War in the First New York Engineers, and joined Carpenters Union No. 1 of Brooklyn in 1868, recalled that the local won the eight-hour day that year and then lost it in the financial crash of 1873. The Baltimore carpenters and untold others also suffered the same fate.

In its infancy, McGuire wrote in *The Carpenter*, October, 1886, the Brotherhood was purely protective in its character, upholding wages and struggling to advance them, but it was always bent upon a movement to shorten the hours of daily toil. At its second convention in 1882, the union urged the adoption of the nine-hour day as a practical first step towards an eight-hour "rule." San Francisco carpenters established the nine-hour day on May 1, 1883, and shortly thereafter, McGuire reported, "wherever there is a local union of Carpenters on the Pacific Slope, not only is nine hours the rule for carpenters, but for all branches of labor in the building line."

In the September, 1884, issue of *The Carpenter*, Edmonston proposed that the Federation of Organized Trades initiate a movement for the eight-hour day. "To depend on the legislative power to adopt this reform" he argued, "is to delay, if not defeat it altogether." On general principles, he declared, he opposed "depending on the ruling class to establish reforms when we can do it ourselves. To concede them a right to pass a law to shorten hours is also to concede the right to lengthen them when the interests of wealth demand." Edmonston also advanced the practical argument that if one state adopted shorter hours, it would give a competitive advantage to neighboring states. He requested the views of his fellow carpenters.

Encouraged by their response, Edmonston moved the question at the Federation's 1884 convention later in the fall, and on his motion, the delegates resolved "that eight hours shall constitute a legal day's labor from and after May 1, 1886." Everyone was asked to join the struggle, but the Knights of Labor refused, a decision that may have contributed to the Knights' subsequent decline and demise.

At the time, the Knights' refusal made some sense. The Federation was in trouble. Its annual income never exceeded $700, and the number of delegates at its annual meetings declined from 107 to a bare handful. (The vote on the eight-hour day proposition was 23 to 2.) As Philip Taft observed, the Federation had little prestige among the international unions, and scarcely any support. The Knights, by far, were more powerful. Despite an acrimonious debate over the future course of the organization between trade unionists and "union haters," those who envisioned an all-embracing organization of farmers, small businessmen and workers, it was growing by leaps and bounds as a consequence of a successful strike of Union Pacific railway shopmen in 1884. Within three years, the Knights' membership skyrocketed from 50,000 to 700,000.

Many carpenters belonged to both the Knights and the Brotherhood. At first, the Brotherhood, particularly McGuire, expressed a cautious willingness to work with the Knights. "Our Brotherhood," McGuire wrote as late as March, 1886, "is not at war with the Knights of Labor, nor are we antagonistic to them. On the contrary, we recognized them as a factor in the labor movement, and we are ever ready to cooperate with them and work in harmony with them as we are ever ready to lend a hand to all branches of honorable toil."

On the local level, however, relations were often strained, as in Washington, D. C., where a faction of the Brotherhood had gone over to the Knights and sought to have all the funds of the local, amounting to $2,300, handed over as an entrance fee to the Knights. In Chicago, relations were exacerbated when Knights assemblies of carpenters offered to work longer and for smaller wages, as the Brotherhood struggled to maintain union rules. The Mitre Assembly of Troy, New York, Knights refused to work with Brotherhood members from nearby Cohoes and refused an exchange of cards proposed by McGuire. By the time the eight-hour movement was underway, the Brotherhood considered the Knights a "dual organization," though not a union.

The refusal of the Knights to join the eight-hour agitation engendered caution among unionists. As Edmonston reported in *The Carpenter*, the 1885 Federation convention thought it best not to order a general enforcement [of the 8-hour resolution] on May 1, 1886, but to assist those who felt strong enough to carry their point. The campaign, as a consequence, was largely left to the local organizations, chiefly in the building trades, among German-speaking furniture workers and cigar-makers in such cities as New York, Chicago, Milwaukee, Cincinnati and Baltimore.

The movement initiated by the carpenters, however, tapped a deep wellspring of emotion on behalf of shorter hours. Union membership rose sharply; the Brotherhood, for example, gained 17,000 new members in 1886. On May 1, over 190,000 workers struck for the eight-hour day. "It was a jolly strike," Oscar Ameringer, then a lad in a Cincinnati furniture factory, wrote in his autobiography, *If You Don't Weaken*. "Victory was dead certain for did not almost everybody belong to the Knights of Labor? Butchers, bakers, and candlestick makers, doctors, preachers, grocerymen and boarding-house keepers. What could be easier? With everybody quitting work the surrender of plutocracy was a foregone conclusion. In addition, there was the union treasury. The first week 'out' married men received six dollars in strike benefits, single men, three. The second week out was not so good. Married men received three dollars and single men nothing. And the third week out all were placed on a basis of American equality, everybody got nothing. . . ."

At first, as Ameringer's spirited account indicates, all went well—at least where the movement was strongest. Then, a bomb burst in Chicago. Club-wielding police broke up an eight-hour rally on May 3 at the McCormick reaper works. Anarchists, who were active among the 10,000 lumber-shovers in the lumber yards, called a protest meeting in Haymarket Square for the next day. A bomb was thrown, wounding 66 policemen (seven died later), the police fired into the crowd, killing several and wounding 200. "The bad news from Chicago fell like an execeedingly cold blanket on us strikers," Ameringer recalled. Eight anarchists were indicted for the bombing, and the public reaction, as Gompers noted, demolished the eight-hour movement and struck at the foundations of the organized labor movement notwithstanding that it had little or nothing to do with anarchism. He also added, "We stood for a fair trial for the underdog whether called anarchist or any other name."

Though there was no evidence linking the anarchists to the bomb, four were hung, one committed suicide in prison, two had their sentences commuted to life, another was sentenced to 15 years' imprisonment. Governor John P. Altgeld subsequently pardoned the latter three.

Yet, the movement for the eight-hour day was not a total loss. Several unions, including the cigarmakers, managed to secure the eight-hour day for their journeymen. In the October 1886 issue of *The Carpenter*, McGuire summarized the extent of the shorter-hours movement among carpenters: "seven of the local unons with 2,486 members are working on the eight-hour system; 17 local unions with 5,824 members are working on the nine-hours plan, and 21 unions have shorter hours of labor on Saturday [making] a sum total of 72,434 hours per week gained to the members by organization. Wages in the trade range from $2 to $3.50 per day, the general average being from $2.25 to $2.50."

As modest as this success may now seem, it encouraged McGuire, Adolph Strasser of the Cigarmakers, Gompers and Edmonston to re-organize the Federation of Organized Trades.

43

A rare photo of Samuel Gompers as he appeared in the late 1880's when William Levi Hutcheson met up with the President of the newly-formed American Federation of Labor for the first time at a Saginaw labor rally.

McGuire drafted the call to a founding congress at Columbus, Ohio, on November 10, 1886. He called the first meeting of the American Federation of Labor to order. Though he refused the temporary chairmanship, he was elected "by acclamation."

"The various trades," states an address by the founders of the A. F. of L., "have been affected by the introduction of machinery, the sub-division of labor, the use of women's and children's labor and the lack of an apprentice system so that the skilled trades were rapidly sinking to the level of pauper labor. To protect the skilled labor of America from being reduced to beggary and to sustain the standard of American workmanship and skill, the trades unions of America have been established."

Sam Gompers was elected President. In recognition of the Carpenters' contribution to the new organization, as well as that of the individuals involved, P. J. McGuire was elected Secretary and Gabriel Edmonston, Treasurer. As Philip Taft points out, the new Federation could only be made a living reality by its permanent officers. The major task, Taft adds, fell on Gompers, the only full-time officer, but he was fortunate in that he could always call upon P. J. McGuire for his advice and assistance. Edmonston, too, with his Washington, D. C. connections, was invaluable as the A. F. of L. sought to become the major voice of organized labor in the country. McGuire not only provided sound advice, but he also placed the strength of the Brotherhood at the disposal of the new Federation. As he reported to the Brotherhood's fifth convention in 1888:

> Wherever a sister labor organization has ever required our help, we have always been ready and willing to grant it. In the great strike of the nailers, our members made it a point to demand union nails with such effect eventually as to secure the settlement of the nailers' strike. . . . our local unions have affiliated with central labor unions, trades assemblies, building trades councils, or other local central bodies of organized labor, wherever they exist, and have formed them in many instances. . . . We have assisted in pushing the growth of the Brotherhood of Painters and Decorators, until it now numbers over 110 unions, and we have given aid in the birth of the International Tin and Sheet-Iron Workers' Association. Both

of these societies have modeled their laws after ours. . . . We have preserved our connection with the American Federation of Labor, that powerful body which now embraces all the leading trades unions of the country, and having a membership of over 550,000, and more than 3000 local societies.

While the Brotherhood remained ever ready to help other sister labor organizations, McGuire also insisted, "In the management of our own trade affairs, we should never make ourselves subordinate to any other organization, nor should we ever allow a dual form to exist in our trade, for if we do, sooner or later, one will be bound to come into conflict with the other to the disadvantage of the workmen's best interests."

The importance of the Brotherhood to the labor movement was underscored when it was chosen to renew the eight-hour day struggle in 1890. * To recover the losses that followed the Haymarket disaster, McGuire proposed a change in tactics. Instead of a general strike of all trades over the issue, he said, let one trade lead the way, then others will be in a position to follow. May 1, 1890 was the date picked for the second test. For as McGuire once explained, "We make it a rule generally . . . that notice should be sent the employers in the month of January and they know that movements cannot be sanctioned by us prior to the first of May."

That year McGuire reported that the movement had been successful in 137 cities, benefiting 46,197 carpenters and countless others in every branch of the building trades. Two years later, he reported a gain of 35 more cities, and that the reduction of the hours of labor had given employment to 15,130 more carpenters, union and non-union men, who would not have been working if the ten-hour day still obtained. By 1900, 186 cities and towns were working under the eight-hour rule. The eight-hour day was on its way to becoming well nigh universal, thanks in considerable measure to the carpenters.

Though the eight-hour struggle enabled the Brotherhood to

---

* Conversely, the labor movement was important to the Brotherhood. The A. F. of L. contributed one-half of its total income in 1890—$12,000—to back the Brotherhood's eight-hour strikes.

Masthead of the original charter

outpace the Knights of Labor carpenter assemblies, its growth was impeded by other rivals, notably the United Order of Carpenters, based primarily in New York City, and the American branches of the English Amalgamated Society of Carpenters and Joiners. Ever generous, McGuire was quick to acknowledge the Brotherhood's debt to the English union, established in 1860. Its exemplary success, he once noted, "was an indication of what might be done in America if a proper organization could be effected."

McGuire, too, was open to cooperation with other woodworker organizations. When the Wood Workers applied for an A. F. of L. charter in 1890, he withdrew his objections on prompting from his colleagues on the Executive Council, though Edmonston later remarked that he could only account for that action because McGuire was "hypnotized by the diplomacy of Thomas Kidd, of the Wood Workers."

In New York City, the United Order of Carpenters erected what the Carpenters called "a wall," a refusal to recognize Brotherhood cards and thereby effectively barring Brotherhood members from jobs in that city. In counterattack, the Brotherhood worked out an exchange of cards with the Amalgamated Society, which had a good foothold in the New York job market, undercutting the Order in its own bailiwick. The Order, in the words of General President D. P. Rowland, "finally agreed to treat with us" and a plan for consolidation was carried out in 1888. The Brotherhood became the United Brotherhood of Carpenters and Joiners of America, 5,000 members richer.

As a consequence of the exchange of cards between the Brotherhood and the Amalgamated Society, the two organizations apparently managed to get along well enough in Chicago and New York, but that was not the case elsewhere. For most of the post-Civil War period, down to the turn of the century, there was a regular trans-Atlantic movement of English carpenters, coming over in the spring and returning in the fall. A carpenter in London earned $9.23 for 51½ hours a week as compared to the New York carpenters' $21 for a 48-hour week. But the "birds-of-passage" were not confined solely to New York City, or even Chicago. In 1900, the Amalgamated Society had 44 U. S. branches, nine in Canada, and about 3,300 members. The Brotherhood opposed the affiliation of the Society with the A. F. of L., but it was admitted in 1891 with the Brotherhood's reluctant consent. In 1901, the Federation's executive council requested that the two organizations change their by-laws so that only one should have jurisdiction in any one city. That proved unworkable, but it was a step towards negotiations over merger.

Others were absorbed—a large number of formerly independent German unions in Chicago, Knights' assemblies, the bulk of the Protective Union of Carpenters in Philadelphia, the Progressive Carpenters and the Sash and Blind-Makers of Brooklyn and the Wood-Peckers Association of New York were among the local unions drawn to the Brotherhood in the 1890s. The Millwrights local in Brooklyn appealed to Brotherhood organizers in millwright centers—Buffalo, Dayton, Akron, Chicago, Milwaukee, Minneapolis and elsewhere—to organize because the Brooklyn bosses talked of getting men from the West for $2.50 per day for ten hours. (The Brooklyn millwrights commanded $3.50 a day for nine hours.)*

The Brotherhood's membership jumped sharply in 1890, a consequence of the shorter hours movement, to peak at 56,937 the following year. The constitution was amended and strengthened, though not without difficulty. The old GEB (General Executive

---

* Millwrights—skilled mechanics having to do with "the unloading, hoisting, dismantling, erecting, assembling, lining and adjusting of all machines used in the transmission of power in buildings, factories or elsewhere, be that power steam, electric, gas, gasoline, water or oil"—were admitted to membership in 1884, and have played a greater role in the Brotherhood's history than their number would suggest. The Toronto, Canada millwrights organized in 1876, affiliating with Local Union 27 in 1884. Harry Lloyd, a pioneer member of the Toronto millwrights, was General President, 1896–1898. James Kirby, General President from 1913 to 1915, was a millwright. The Associated Millwrights of America, headquartered in Buffalo, New York, joined the Brotherhood in 1930. In the late 1940s, there were some 21 Millwright locals with a membership of 5,347 and 947 local unions with millwright members. In 1914, the International Association of Machinists challenged the Brotherhood's jurisdiction over the millwrights, provoking what must be the longest running jurisdiction quarrel in the history of American labor. It was resolved in 1954. (See page 95.)

Board) elected by local unions in the immediate vicinity of the national office, was no longer representative, nor workable. The new constitution, adopted in 1890, provided for two vice-presidents, no longer required to be organizers, and a GEB elected by the convention from seven districts around the country. (The convention recommendations were at first turned down by referendum, but the key sections restructuring the GEB were adopted seriatum in a subsequent referendum. Opponents had claimed that the new GEB would be too costly.) Dues were raised to 50 cents and the per capita tax to 15 cents. Strike benefits were set at $6 a week.

"The United Brotherhood," McGuire informed the delegates at the 1890 convention with reason, "is in the front ranks of labor organizations . . . its growth is unparalleled . . . An immense work has been accomplished. We have spread the gospel of unionism . . . in every town and hamlet . . . and have inspired a spirit of noble and sturdy manhood among the carpenters which . . . will brook none of the impositions and wrongs of old."

Yet, the carpenters' spirit was endangered—by economic catastrophe and by technological change. The panic of 1893 cut the Brotherhood's membership by almost one-half in two years. Harrisburg Local 287 loaned 50 cents to out-of-work members towards keeping dues paid. By the end of the year, the local had to drop sick benefits, local officers served six months without pay, and the Brotherhood had to exempt the local from paying its per capita for two months. The Harrisburg local was not alone in its financial gloom.

One consequence: when the Brotherhood polled its locals, at the behest of the A. F. of L., on the immigration question, quite a large number favored entire suspension of immigration until all wage workers in this country had employment. McGuire proposed the suspension of immigration for one year, but the A. F. of L. executive council voted against endorsing the proposal. He was active on a Federation committee that ultimately recommended mild restrictions on the lines of an educational test and favored stricter enforcement of measures to guard against entrance of criminal or pauper elements. Along with most of the labor movement, the Brotherhood was opposed to Oriental immigration, holding with Gompers that it involved the larger question of racial preservation and that Oriental workers "have driven white workers out, have established conditions and wages that are incompatible with American standards of work and life."

But the gravest threat to the carpenters was that of technological change. As R. M. Stender, Santa Barbara Local 1062 member, wrote in the January, 1927 issue of *The Carpenter*, the 1880s saw the coming of concrete building, among other things. "I who had been a builder and framer became, save the mark, a form-builder. I erected staging for other craftsmen, was often deluged with water, and had my tool-box filled with the same, and, generally speaking, became a mere 'handy man' on the job."

"Year after year," McGuire reported in 1894, "carpenter work is becoming less and less plentiful owing to recent innovations in architectural construction. With the introduction of iron and steel frames in the larger buildings, with iron and stone stair cases, tile floors and tile or metal wainscoting, with cornices and bay windows in many cases of other material than wood and with numerous other changes going on . . . the increase and perfection of wood-working machinery, the chances of steady employment of carpenters are extremely uncertain."

"So it ranges," he informed the United States Industrial Commission in 1899, "tiling, grooving and flooring, all through the manifold branches of woodwork, there is from three to fifteen times as much product as there was formerly by hand; and the machines are operated in most instances by unskilled labor at low wages—$1 to $1.20 a day. In Oshkosh, mainly, the machines are tended by girls, and in those other towns . . . in the Northwest, girls less than twelve and thirteen years of age, some of them as low as ten and eleven, work for fifty to sixty cents a day; and every third one you will find minus some of the digits of their hands."

The Brotherhood responded by organizing the mills with a new weapon—the boycott. The first boycott began in 1896 when the Brotherhood cautioned New York builders, architects and manufacturers of trim work against awarding "further contracts to outside firms as, unless proof is given that the trim has been constructed under strict union rules, they would at any time refuse to handle it." With the aid of the New York City Building Trades Council, which called sympathetic strikes whenever non-union carpenters were employed to install unfair trim, the boycott rapidly became effective. These methods, reports Leo Wolman in his study of the boycott, effectively eliminated non-uinion building trim from the New York market. He also concluded that by the effective application of the boycott, the Brotherhood "laid the foundation for what was later to develop into one of the strongest labor organizations in this country."

The boycott was backed by a sound but cautious strike strategy. Strikes were not sanctioned by the executive board, i.e., there would be no strike benefits, unless the local or district council president had appointed a three-man committee to adjust the dispute with employers. Should that effort fail, a strike had to be approved by a two-thirds vote in a secret ballot of the members present at a meeting called on a week's notice. Then a detailed account must be sent to the General Secretary. If necessary, the GEB deputized one of its number to attempt to adjudicate the dispute. Any local or district council engaging in a strike without the consent of the executive board was liable to expulsion (a penalty rarely—if ever—enforced). Any member scabbing was subject to a fine or expulsion or both. However, the locals were free to cope with non-union conditions as circumstances warranted. As William L. Hutcheson once reminded carpenters, "We have to depend on you boys to carry on conditions. If you find non-union conditions prevailing in violation of your trade rules, don't waste time getting in touch with the General office. Get them off."

Discipline paid off. McGuire reported in 1898 that since 1883 the union had expended $354,293 in support of trade disputes. "In that period," he added, "we have had 1,026 strikes and lockouts, of which 998 were successful, 61 were lost, and 67 compromised." By then, according to McGuire, wages were up 50 cents a day over what they were before the union started in 70 percent of the cities under the union's jurisdiction. In 1904, Edmonston noted a general advance in wages over the history of the union from $1.50 a day to an average of double that amount. Brotherhood members were forbidden to lump, subcontract or accept piece-work on pain of a fine of not less than $10 nor more than $50, effectively abolishing piecework. The union adopted a union label in 1900, providing that it was to be issued to shops that complied with the conditions and trade rules of their respective localities and that paid a minimum wage of at least 25 cents an hour.

By the end of the century, the Brotherhood reached a high of 68,463 members in good standing. This, despite "panic," depression losses of 28,000 in 1894–1895. Of the 679 local unions chartered as of July 1, 1900, there were 40 working in the German language, 6 French, 2 Bohemian, 2 Jewish, 1 Scandinavian, 1 "'Latin,'" and 16 locals in the South of colored carpenters. In distinctive trade branches, there were 9 mill men's locals, 6 stair builders' locals, 1 car builders' local and 1 floor layers' local. The Brotherhood had not only survived, but it was now one of the strongest trade unions in the country.

Unhappily, McGuire's life ended in tragedy. As is sometimes the case with charismatic men, McGuire was not a good administrator. In any event, the union had grown too fast and too large for one person to manage. Over the years, McGuire had been in the habit of digging into his own pocket to pay his expenses and even pledged his personal credit whenever it went into the hole. Moreover, the Brotherhood's money was banked under McGuire's name until February 1901. Neither practice was sound even when necessary and even though approved by convention and executive board action.

As day-to-day union management became too much for McGuire, he became ill and began to drink too much. When William D. Huber became president in 1899, he found that he could not work with McGuire. "I found the office in deplorable condition," he reported to the executive board early in 1901. In April an audit uncovered a shortage of $6,300, later, a little over $10,000. No one ever believed that he had embezzled the money. As Gompers later wrote to Frank Duffy, "I did not believe, and do not now believe that he was intentionally dishonest and any shortage in his account was brought about by the awful mental strain and responsibility devolving upon him during the years of struggle in behalf of the Brotherhood, and of the general labor movement." Unfortunately, it was clear that P. J. McGuire had to go.

It was no easy task. McGuire was a hero to carpenters and to many others within the labor movement. They would hear no ill of McGuire, not even that he was too sick to carry out his duties. "I was looked upon with holy horror," Frank Duffy, who had to assume McGuire's responsibilities, wrote to Gompers, "and it got to such a pitch that certain individuals would not take a drink with me, nor even a smoke." Gompers was so concerned that he sent Frank Morrison, then Secretary-Treasurer of the A. F. of L., to Philadelphia to see what could be done. So that the union might sue the bonding company for recovery of the money, McGuire had to suffer arrest and indictment as an embezzler. To clear his name, he appeared before the 1902 convention, hair white at age 50, bent with arthritic pain, afflicted with dropsy and gastric catarrh. Throwing himself upon the mercy of the convention, he called upon the delegates' sense of fairness. "I do not care whether I sink or swim," he said, "so long as this organization is maintained."

By a vote of 198 for and 137 against, McGuire's resignation was accepted. He had paid the union $1,000 in settlement of all claims against him. The criminal charges were dropped. McGuire died the night of February 18, 1906. His last words, spoken in delirium, were: "I've got to get to California. The boys in Local 22 need me."

McGuire's career began, as a resolution of the A. F. of L. executive council remarked, "at a time when it was almost considered a disgrace to be a participant in the labor movement." He was a pioneer, the resolution continued, "who blazed the way on this North American Continent for the great army of organized labor . . . We found him at all times an earnest, efficient and valiant co-worker in the cause of labor. His ability was very great, certainly none in the movement were more able, and few were his equals."

P. J. McGuire was not only a founder of the Brotherhood, he was the architect of the labor movement. During the twenty years he served so selflessly as Secretary of the union, he was ever ready to offer his astute and vigorous services to others in organizing workers in other crafts and callings as well as in negotiations with their employers. Gompers, who knew him from boyhood, described McGuire as a man "of rare gifts and quality of nature and character."

An Upholder of Cheap Bosses and Low Wages.

What his old friend termed "his splendid attaintments" are embodied in the living institutions that make up the labor movement.

On McGuire's death, W. J. Shields, General President in 1886–1888, wrote: "He understood that the trade union movement was a great democratic training schoool of the workers, where not only parliamentary procedure is taught, but the method of trade union necessity in its deep, simple sense."

That understanding was McGuire's greatest gift to his fellow workers.

IV

ONE ORGANIZATION . . .
ONE TRADE

Though troubled by the McGuire tragedy, the Brotherhood entered the new century with a certain euphoria. In the first three years, it organized more carpenters than in two decades of strenuous effort, with membership rising sharply from 31,508 in 1898 to 161,217 in 1903–1904. As a jubilant president, William D. Huber told the delegates at the union's 1904 convention in Milwaukee, "after nearly a quarter century of struggles and privations on the part of its members [the Brotherhood] emerges as an organization second to none."

This growth, as may be imagined, was a source of satisfaction to carpenter unionists, but not one for complacency. It was, rather, as General Secretary Frank Duffy noted, "an incentive . . . to carry on the good work of organization until we have every man working at the trade within our ranks, be he carpenter or joiner, stairbuilder, shipjoiner, millwright, planing mill bench hand, cabinet maker, car builder or engaged in running wood-working machinery."

The union was reaching out, a development that most found a challenge, but some found worrisome. Growth caused some internal strain and created enemies. "Never before in the history of our organization," Duffy declared in his 1904 convention report, "have we had to contend with so much opposition from our employers. . ." The era of the anti-labor injunction had just begun,

R.E.L. Connolly,
2nd Gen. V. Pres., 1902

T. Guerin,
1st Gen. V. Pres., 1902

Wm. D. Huber,
Gen. Pres., 1902

and the Brotherhood was a major target. The Panic of 1905; recessions, in 1907–1908 and, again, in 1910–1912; these severely cropped the growth of the union. For all its rosy-hued dawn, the century's first decade was a difficult one for the Brotherhood.

For fifty-year-old William D. Huber, it was a trying time. He had to cope not only with problems created by growth but also with those left by the charismatic and, towards the end, erratic leadership of P. J. McGuire. Born in Waterloo, New York, on June 13, 1852, Huber was an experienced carpenter and trade unionist. He served his apprenticeship in Corning, New York, where his parents had moved and he attended school. At age 20, he went to Canisteo, New York, where he went to work for a wood-working firm, said to be the largest in the state. After four years, he became a foreman, a post he held until he left for New York City some six years later. Eventually settling in Yonkers, he became a charter member of Local 726 and remained proud to the end of his days that he had filled every office within the gift of the Local. At the tenth Brotherhood convention in New York City in 1898, he was elected first General Vice-President unanimously, in recognition of his services which included leadership of the struggle for the eight-hour day in the New York area. When John Williams resigned on October 18, 1899, he became General President of the Brotherhood. In 1905 he became a vice president of the American Federation of Labor, a post he held until his resignation from the presidency of the Brotherhood in 1912. He died on September 12, 1925.

Huber's photographs reflect a rugged determination behind a high forehead and full mustache. A contemporary wrote, "He is now popularly known as 'honest old Bill,' a name well suited to him, for, whether friend or enemy, it makes no difference to him: he treats all alike." These are qualities he surely needed as he confronted the challenges of his day.

At the 1902 Atlanta convention, the delegates amended the constitution to give the General President additional authority, including the appointment and assignment (at local request) of organizers, the examination of local rules and by-laws for conformity to the constitution, the signing of charters, and power to decide "all points of law, and all grievances and appeals, except as to disapproved claims, subject to an appeal to the G.E.B." The General Secretary-Treasurer post was divided and a first and second vice president named. (Frank Duffy, Thomas Neale,* T. M. Guerin and H. Fuller, respectively, filled these offices for most of the century's first decade.) The delegates also established a seven-member General Executive Board, one elected from each of seven divisions—the Northeast, the Middle-Atlantic states, the South, the Midwest, Northwest, West and Canada. The union was growing geographically as well as numerically, including the carpenters of Puerto Rico, where Santiago Iglesias had been active organizing for the Brotherhood and the A. F. of L. since 1904,† and those in the Canal Zone soon after. (At the insistence of some border locals in Texas, the Brotherhood considered including Mexico within its jurisdiction, but the effort apparently never made much headway.) The G.E.B. met quarterly to authorize strike sanctions, hear benefit appeals and review reports of the General President and the other general officers.

The standing of the general officers with the board, unfortunately, was not made clear. They could speak before it (the President had to submit a quarterly report) but had no vote. For the most part, the board met without their presence and, increasingly, the officers appeared only when summoned. It was awkward, and, towards the end of the Huber presidency, became a source of

* Thomas Neale was born in England in 1869 where he learned the carpenter trade by following in his father's footsteps. He came to this country in 1888, landing first in Toronto, Canada, then moving to Pittsburgh where he joined Local Union 142. He moved to Chicago in 1891, becoming secretary-treasurer of the Chicago District Council in 1898, just in time to participate in the great building trades lockout of 1899. Elected General Treasurer at the Atlanta convention, he served the Brotherhood in the post until his death in 1941.

† Santiago Iglesia, a native of Corunna, Spain, who was an apprenticed cabinet maker at age 12, joined the Brotherhood in New York City in 1900. A year later, A. F. of L. President Sam Gompers sent him to Puerto Rico as an organizer. He founded and edited three labor periodicals, became a member of the Puerto Rican Senate from 1917 to 1932, was elected Resident Commissioner in 1932 and 1936, and represented the island in Congress. He died on December 4, 1940, still active in the labor movement as an official of the Pan-American Labor Federation.

conflict. The strained relations between the board and the general officers was behind his resignation in 1912 and prompted Duffy's remark to the 1912 convention: "Things are not altogether smooth underneath the surface; we are not working in harmony in this organization. We are split and divided, and it is a mystery to me that we grow and prosper under these conditions."

One reason, of course, was the overall soundness of the union. "When we consider the great benefits that we have derived from our union" Milton N. Rogers wrote in a letter to *The Carpenter* in July, 1906, "we must come to the conclusion that it pays to belong to a labor union." "Today," Rogers added, Minneapolis Local 7 "is in better condition in every way than ever before . . . It is grand and powerful. We have about 1,500 members, a well-filled treasury, harmony and solidarity in our ranks."

Most carpenters, apparently, shared Rogers' elation; their union was a grand brotherhood. But they did not always see eye to eye on the issues affecting its fate. When the 1902 convention decided to move the union's headquarters from Philadelphia to Indianapolis, some delegates were opposed on the grounds that "the large majority of our membership will be found east of the Ohio River."* (The 1908 decision to buy land and build headquarters of their own was widely acclaimed. The Ironworkers and Teamsters were among the several unions that rented space from the Brotherhood when the building was completed in 1909. Indianapolis served as a union center for a half-century thereafter with the Carpenters serving as "landlord" to the movement.)

---

* Though the decision to move to Indianapolis was one for growth, the argument for it was couched in terms of savings to the union. On travel time for board members, for example, at a cost of 3 cents a mile, it was estimated that the union would save $720 a year. Indianapolis, then a few miles from the center of population of the United States, was also a major rail center of sixteen railroads with an average of one hundred mail trains every twenty-four hours, going and coming. To quote the majority report, "To send a letter to Philadelphia from the Pacific Coast and receive an answer requires at least twelve days; to perform the same service between Eastern points and Indianapolis requires but four days. [The same applied to the South and Southwest.] The progress of some of the Local Unions on the Pacific Coast has been greatly hindered, owing to the fact that they were unable to get the necessary advice from the General Office in time to enable them to adjust their difficulties."

When President Huber in 1903 appointed a black organizer, a Brother Burgess, to work in the South, *The Carpenter* was flooded with correspondence, pro and con, for months afterward. It was, incidentally, a courageous decision on the part of the Brotherhood in the heyday of the Ku Klux Klan. Local unions in the South were organized along race lines for racialist reasons rather than because of discrimination, at least in the view of the Brotherhood's leadership and that of the membership outside the South where local unions were often ethnically organized.† Some opposition to the appointment of Brother Burgess was clearly racist. As one letter writer phrased it, "It is useless for any one to think that the African will ever be placed on the same social scale as the Anglo-Saxon." Surprisingly, to a northerner looking back from this point in time, there was support for Burgess' appointment from Southern white carpenters. Much of this support was pragmatic. As a fellow carpenter (white) wrote from Savannah, where Burgess had been president of Local 318, "we are always in competition with them . . . because [contractors] can get them cheap. In [Savannah] we have three hundred white carpenters and five hundred negro carpenters, and the latter have less unemployed than the whites. The reason is that they are not well organized and can be hired for less wages. So I say we must organize them; for if we can afford to work all day on a scaffold beside them we can surely afford to meet them in the hall for an hour or so once in a while." As a pragmatist, the writer was of the opinion that a white organizer would do better among blacks than a black one, but he was willing to stand by the union's decision, for, as he pointedly added, "the mere fact that all

† See organizer E. J. Dyer's report from Manitoba of September, 1906:

I have just received a request from fifty German carpenters who are anxious to start a German union and, encouraged by the success of French Local No. 1688, I have called a meeting for August 14 and hope to have a strong local by the time this is in the hands of the members. I am sorry to have to depart from the well-defined plan of concentration in one big local, but I have found it impossible to get these foreigners in. I may yet have to form a Swedish and Norwegian union also, as I believe there is at present fully one hundred of them at work in the city and only about ten in the union. I feel that by organizing them separately we can better educate the men and concentrate their forces into one organization later.

Construction of Union Headquarters in Indianapolis, completed in 1909.

of the boss builders in the South are advocating leaving the negroes out of the unions is a good reason why we should organize them." "Let the good work go on," he concluded, "and let us hope for the day when there will be equal rights to all and special privileges to none."

This was in the spirit of the Brotherhood; as a June, 1903 statement on the question in *The Carpenter* put it:

> Our General Constitution does not contain any provision justifying our General President in making any discrimination as to color, race or creed in his appointments. And while it is true that Brother Burgess has been appointed as an organizer for our colored brothers in particular, it would be unwise and in conflict with our laws and principles to debar him for organizing white men of our craft when an opportunity presents itself.
>
> We are banded together in our grand Brotherhood for the purpose of elevating the condition of our entire craft, regardless of color, nationality, race or creed. Prejudice on these lines has no standing in the labor movement, and we cannot consistently deny admittance in our organization to any man because he belongs to the African race, which, as we well know, is very numerous in the Southern States. Here it is the negro who must receive our closest attention; he must be brought into our fold in order that his hours of toil be reduced and his wages raised, and thus his white brother will be given an opportunity to raise his own standing to the level of his brother in the East and West.
>
> In many instances white men are called on to work with negroes on buildings or in shops, and they do so without raising any objection. Now, if such is the case, why should they object to meeting the negro in their Local Unions and placing them under the control of the organization as a safeguard against unfair competition?
>
> In this connection we mention an incident which recently occurred in Atlantic City. A negro employer there, perfectly willing to work union hours and to pay union wages, found it impossible to secure union labor because the Local Union of that city refused admittance to the colored carpenter, and its members at the same time refused to work for the employer because he was a negro.
>
> In Birmingham, Ala., the colored carpenters, anxious to become members of the United Brotherhood and abide by its trade-rules, were refused admittance by the Local Union, nor would the Union

render them any assistance in organizing a Local of their own, and strange as it may appear, they were organized by Union hod-carriers, who were less prejudiced and narrow-minded than our own members. Such actions are discreditable to our Brotherhood, and we say that, however difficult a task the elimination of race prejudice may be, as far as our Brotherhood is concerned the drawing of the color line should be stopped at once and for all time.

As the Brotherhood expanded, the problems it faced became more complex. When P. J. McGuire, in 1881, first "became convinced of the absolute necessity of organizing a society of journeymen carpenters and joiners, thoroughly American in character and as broad as the land in which we live, embracing all men of the trade regardless of race, creed, color or politics," little or no consideration was given to organizing mills manufacturing materials for the construction industry.* Some were organized in the late 1890's. In 1904, President Huber declared the mill question "one of the most knotty and intricate problems that confront our Brotherhood today."

The industry was changing—rapidly. As *The Carpenter* noted, in 1902, "The industrial transitions of the past two decades have entirely effaced the former lines of demarcation between the various branches. . . . The cabinetmaker for instance is almost exclusively engaged in the construction of building trim, the machine wood worker is doing half the work formerly done by the carpenter by hand and later on by machine. Thus, cabinetmakers or mill-hands and machine hands both, have become carpenters and are entitled to carpenters' wages and carpenters' hours." Huber, in decrying those outside carpenters who had no use for the millhands, viewing them as a drag on journeymen carpenters, pointedly remarked, "the

* Note the changes in the trade or craft qualifications for membership over the years: The first Constitution published in 1882 specified only carpenters or joiners "of good moral character;" by 1886 stair builders, millwrights, planing mill bench hands or cabinet makers engaged at carpenter work, or any carpenter running wood-working machinery were admitted; by 1902 the Brotherhood added an age qualification, not less than twenty-one and not over fifty years of age, and ship joiners, car-builders (workers building "all wooden railroad and sheet cars" or providing the finish on *all* cars, wood or hollow metal).

carpenter today may be the millman of tomorrow." To hold what rightfully belongs to him, Huber declared, the carpenter must control the manufacture of the material.

Organization of the mills entailed combatting child labor as organizer R. Fuelle graphically reported from Dubuque, Iowa, where five hundred millmen went on strike for union recognition and the nine-hour day on April 12, 1907. The mills were shut down for twelve days, then re-opened and the Brotherhood was hit by an injunction. Meanwhile, a state investigation launched at the instigation of the Brotherhood uncovered children of twelve employed at $2.50 to $3.00 a week. "In one factory," Fuelle wrote, "eighteen children were found by the labor commissioner. In former years, when that officer came into the front door, the children were chased out the rear. This time, however, we got the drop on them unexpectedly." The companies were fined and forced to dismiss the children, but the strike went on for over thirty weeks. Fuelle urged, "Every one of our members should use his best efforts to make the fight a success. It will do away forever with child slavery in our craft in the mill industry."

On January 2, 1905, William D. Haywood, head of the Western Federation of Miners, founded the Industrial Workers of the World, the famed Wobblies, an industrial union. For some carpenters, the Wobblies proved to be another radical chimera. Globe, Arizona carpenters, for example, were so beguiled by the dream of industrial unionism that in 1906 they called upon the Brotherhood to affiliate with the new group. The G.E.B., however, promptly declared the IWW "a dual union," and President Huber reflected the 1906 convention majority when he charged the Wobblies with fomenting "division and enmity . . . . a few fool dreamers who, hiding their nefarious designs and hypocrisy under the guise of organized principles, now ordain and declare that trades unions, as presently formed, are ages behind the times, and boast that our unions must succumb to the inevitable and be disrupted, divided and torn apart."

While the IWW did appeal to certain workers, notably immigrant factory workers in the Northeast and migrant farm and lumber workers in the West, it had little attraction for carpenters.

Child labor collecting their wages.

Few, if any, left the Brotherhood to join the Wobblies. Interestingly enough, the Brotherhood's abhorrence of dual unionism did not prevent it from urging support when Wobbly rights, as workers, were violated. In Lawrence, Massachusetts, during a Wobbly-led textile strike in 1912, a woman striker was shot and killed, another striker was framed for planting dynamite, and two strike leaders were indicted for murder of the young woman. In San Diego, the police hounded Wobbly soap-boxers off the streets and vigilantes joined in the harassment. While expressing little sympathy for the IWW as a dual organization and deploring their sometimes provocative tactics, *The Carpenter* of June, 1912 made the point: "It should be remembered that they and their sympathizers and their acts are part of the workers' struggle for better conditions." Noting that members of the A. F. of L. unions were also persecuted, the editorial voiced the Brotherhood's indignation at the lawless and brutal conduct of the authorities and urged that members "hold protest meetings and use their influence in every way possible to the end that workingmen and women are fully protected and not interfered with in the exercise of their constitutional rights, that the men under indictment are accorded a fair trial and law and order again prevail in these cities."

Matters were further complicated by jurisdictional challenges from the Wood, Wire & Metal Lathers' International Union and the Sheetmetal Workers, among others. They stemmed from the move away from wood to other materials in construction, especially in the larger cities. As the Secretary-Treasurer of the Greater New York District Council, D. F. Featherstone wrote to *The Carpenter* in April, 1909, in response to the new building codes, "wood in office buildings bids fair to become as extinct as the Dodo." Hollow steel doors and trim had supplanted wood, he added, "and we are the sufferers."

The New York City carpenters, however, won arbitration cases involving the new materials—kalamine (wood sheathed in metal), steel trim and even a plaster-like substance, elignum, used briefly as fire-proofing. At the 1910 convention, New York delegates demonstrated, using the tools of the trade and the new materials, how they proved the new material to be carpenters' work. "You can cut that metal with any old saw," the New York delegate explained, but to install kalamine, "you must have the carpenter with his tools to do the work." He next demonstrated how steel trim could be cut in a woodmiter box and pointed out that steel trim was replacing kalamine in office buildings and large apartment houses. He showed how the new metal-covered doors were hung in an iron jamb: "On this side you see an ordinary wooden screw and on this side a machine screw. It is set with a plumb rule and plumb bob the same as you would set a wooden jam." As far as the sheet metal worker claim of trim went, he said, "I can't see where he fits in at all. You don't take his snips, nor his soldering iron, nor anything at all that the sheet metal worker uses. You don't use any of his skill or art. You confine yourself to the skill of the carpenter and you use the carpenter's tools and none other."

The New York victories led the way and the Brotherhood soon established its right to trim work elsewhere. One reason the carpenters won was that employers found themselves calling in carpenters to rectify the imperfect hanging of metal covered doors within steel jambs by inexperienced sheet metal workers. But this did not altogether halt the piracy of carpenters' work, which was rooted in employers' hopes that they could get work done by $1.50-a-day men rather than by carpenters at $2 a day. One consequence was fragmentation of the trade. "Organizations have sprung into existence during the last few years," Frank Duffy declared at the 1904 convention, "that were never dreamed or thought of by the founders of trade unions. These organizations have been pirating away parts of our trade until it became unbearable." Locomotive Wood Workers, the Agricultural Wood Workers, the Railway Bridge Builders, Millwrights, Shinglers, Dock, Wharf and Bridge Builders, Metal Ceiling Wood Workers and Carpenters' Helpers were among those seeking A. F. of L. charters in 1903 and 1904. The Brotherhood's protests, however, headed off a Federation comprised of tiny, ineffectual unions fragmented by marginal craft skills.

Fragmentation was not the only danger. Jurisdictional erosion raised the spectre of ultimate dissolution. President Huber hammered the point home at the 1910 convention: "Something must be done or it's only a question of a decade or two until the carpenter craft will be such in name only, and our membership will gradually disseminate and affiliate itself with some special branch, which is simply the child or offspring, so to speak, of the carpenter industry."

In an effort to clarify lines of jurisdiction within the construction industry, the Brotherhood took the lead in 1903 in organizing the Structural Building Trades Alliance. Duffy served as temporary chairman; John Kirby, president of the Carpenters Chicago District Council, became first vice president of the group. The Alliance staked out eight basic jurisdictions—the Carpenters, wood; the Bricklayers, masonry; the Plumbers, pipe-fitting; the Painters, decorating; the Plasterers, plastics; the Bridge and Structural Iron Workers, iron; the Hoisting Engineers, motive power, the Hod Carriers, common laborers. Jurisdictional disputes were to be handled by the central organization based upon equal representation at conventions from each of the eight international unions. Local Alliances were established to support striking member unions by sympathetic walkouts after approval by a two-thirds majority and by the international unions involved. As historian Philip Taft pointed out, the Alliance did not generate much enthusiasm in the A. F. of L. There was some fear that the Alliance might go its own way. As a consequence, the leaders of the Alliance and the A. F. of L. agreed on a program to bring the building trades unions into a structrual group under the aegis of the Federation. The A. F. of L. Building Trades Department was founded in February, 1908. The Alliance then dissolved.

What the Brotherhood hoped to achieve through an effective Building Trades Department and with the organization of local building trades councils was illustrated in Calgary, Canada. After a successful walkout against the employment of non-union carpenters, the Calgary local of the Brotherhood decided to give the newly organized Teamsters union a hand. They had been working eleven to thirteen hours a day for $35-$45 a month and went on strike in June, 1903 for a $50-a month wage. The Calgary carpenters decided to stop handling lumber delivered by scabs. They were locked out, and were joined by construction laborers refusing to handle scab-delivered lime or sandstone. But stonemasons and bricklayers refused to recognize the sympathy strike. Stonemasons were making $4 a day compared to the carpenter's $2.50. Contractors were able to recruit homesteaders and others able to handle a hammer and saw, Warren Caragata reports in his brief history, *Alberta Labour*. MacKenzie King "arbitrated" a settlement that allowed contractors, as a dispatch carried in the Toronto *Globe* phrased it, to "employ whom they like, there is no discrimination between the union and non-union men." The back of the strike was broken, the Calgary Carpenters' charter was withdrawn, and the union was not reorganized until a year later. An effective building trades council might have averted the disaster.

Though the Carpenters played a leading role in establishing the Department, the Brotherhood's relationship with it, to say the least, was a touchy one. As a consequence of a clash over jurisdiction with U.S. sheet metal workers, the Department suspended the Carpenters and, in January 1911, asked that the Carpenters' charter be revoked by the Federation. Unaccustomed to hasty solutions of jurisdictional disputes, as Phillip Taft put it, the Federation delayed taking action. Pushed by the Building Department, the A. F. of L. Executive Council, in a decision upheld by the 1911 Federation convention, declared that the suspension of charters was primarily the responsibility of the American Federation of Labor; the revocation of charters was not an effective method of solving jurisdictional disputes. The Department was asked to reinstate the suspended union. "Clearly," Taft concluded, "the Federation was not prepared automatically to endorse a policy which, in a large sense, was antipathetic to the spirit of the A. F. of L.—a policy in this case fraught with peril for the entire labor movement."

Certainly it was not wise policy at a time when labor faced constant harassment in the courts and at the hands of "the employing interests." In the struggle to organize, the union label—(adopted by the Carpenters in 1900) became increasingly important—as did the boycott: the refusal of union men either to handle non-union materials or to work alongside non-union men. In 1902, the American Anti-Boycott Association was established "to eradicate the sympathetic strike and the boycott against non-union materials and to establish industrial peace and the principles of personal

When building tradesmen began restoring the White House in Washington, D.C., in 1949, they removed an old panel from the East Room, and on the back of the panel they discovered the early Carpenters' union label, shown above. Since the United Brotherhood's label was not officially adopted until 1900, it is assumed that the label on the panel was installed during the remodeling process which Congress authorized in 1902. As the picture shows, the label bears No. 4569. Although the number is indistinct, it appears to have been issued to "Factory No. 10, Bronx, N.Y."

liberty . . . ." So-called Citizens Alliances sprang up throughout the country to push the open shop and to buck up employer resistance to unionization. They were encouraged by the likes of David M. Parry, head of the National Association of Manufacturers, who declared that organized labor "knows but one law . . . the law of physical force—the law of the Huns and Vandals, the law of the savage."

The lockout, injunction, importation of scabs, and the yellow-dog contract were among the consequences of what the Carpenters called "Parryism." When Waterbury, Connecticut carpenters refused to work with non-union men and to sign an open-shop agreement, employers declared a lockout that lasted three-and-one-half years. When the carpenters of Billings, Montana sought the eight-hour day in 1906 at the former nine-hour rate of $4, the Citizens Alliance organized the opposition. Carpenters, painters, lathers, bricklayers, stonemasons, plasterers, laborers and teamsters refused to work for non-union contractors. James Curran, president, and W. P. Andrews, recording secretary, of Local Union 1172, described what happened in the October, 1906 *Carpenter:* "In this way affairs went on for some time, many of the union carpenters contracting all the work they could obtain, in order to keep the union men employed. Then, the non-union contractors began to ship in men. Some of the latter joined the union, some left town and others went to work on unfair jobs. These men were to receive 50 cents per hour and to work nine hours per day; a good many being paid less, however. . . . A good many of the union men have left town, only about fifty or sixty men remaining here of a membership of 187 last spring."

In Ithaca, New York, *The Carpenter* reported, "the mill owners have notified all their employees that they must sign individual agreements [Yellow-Dog contracts] by January 1, 1906, or be discharged." The Brotherhood local countered with a demand for the eight-hour day, and shut down the mills. Elsewhere, carpenters picketed railroad stations to warn off men attracted by Citizens' Alliance employment bureaus, or recruiting stations. Alliance adherents in Musgrove, Indian Territory, organizer J. W. Adams reported in the July 1905 *Carpenter*, imported "a lot of men to take the places of those locked out [but] all . . . who were mechanics came to our headquarters, and upon learning the true conditions, refused to go to work. Our boys paid their fare back to their homes."

The Brotherhood was not without its own resources to counter employer lockouts. In 1905, G.E.B. Chairman William Schardt called on the general manager of the Fuller Construction Company to inform him that unless a New York lockout was settled, the carpenters employed by the company in Chicago would also be called out.

The first injunction experienced by carpenters, at least the first reported in *The Carpenter*, in 1903, was a foretaste of the broadscale attack mounted against American labor by employers in the early decades of this century. "We were successful," First General Vice President T.M. Guerin wrote, in a report on a mill-men's strike in Rochester, New York, "in getting most of our men to work and the outside contractors to agree to handle none but union trim." The employers, he added, "were so cast down at the failure of their efforts "to destroy our organization . . . that they resorted to the courts of assistance. *The indictment covers everything that is of value to trade unionism.*" (Italics added.) The president of Local Union 72 and the District Council, the Carpenters' business agent, and

Guerin were indicted for the part they played in the strike. The charges against the union were: Refusal to work with non-union men, refusal to handle non-union material, asking men to join the union, trying to raise wages to $2.25 a day, getting outside businessmen to buy only fair material, not patronizing firms who employed non-union men, and as Guerin added, in fact everything from breathing fresh air to paying funeral benefits to the widow of a union man. The employers also instituted damage suits of $50,000 against the Rochester Brotherhood locals.

As it turned out, the Carpenters ultimately won that case, spending altogether—on Rochester and other similar cases—some $395. But that was the merest foretaste. (The Rochester strike cost, in donations, $3,300.)* In 1908, Huber reported handling twenty-eight law cases, winning eleven, losing six (the rest pending), at a cost of $12,304. For the two years ending in June, 1910, injunctions and civil-suit costs mounted to $19,203; and two years later, to $33,450.

"Show me an injunction granted," Huber declared in the September, 1910 *Carpenter*, "and I will show you one more link forged in the chain of 'open shop' dogma." When the trades working upon New York's famed St. John the Divine Cathedral threatened to quit over the installation of non-union trim encasing the organ, the American Anti-Boycott Association secured an injunction on behalf of Irving & Casson, the Massachusetts decorative wood firm involved. The Irving & Casson injunction barred, among other things, carpenters from informing others—architects, builders and other craft unionists—that the company was "unfair," though the judge did strike out of the draft order the phrase, "to each other," presumably leaving carpenters free to tell each other about the

---

* The Rochester strike donation was in the middling range for the two years 1903/1904. The Brotherhood spent $47,000 in New York City, a special case involving what Frank Duffy called "a family fight," a fight between the Amalgamated Society and the Brotherhood, and $100 for a strike or lockout in Oil City, Pa. The next largest expenditure to New York's was $8,500 in aid of striking Philadelphians. It also spent $4,600 in support of Montreal, Canada carpenters; $5,000 in Toronto; $2,200 in Omaha; $1,820 in Spokane; $1,186 in Mobile; and $1,250 in San Diego.

facts. The Brotherhood further succeeded in having the order amended so that other workers could go out "voluntarily," though the Brotherhood could not call them out in sympathy, and left the union free to strike for good cause and free to fine its own members should they work on non-union trim. Of such stuff were union victories made in the dark days of the injunction.

"Experience," *The Carpenter* declared in November, 1902, "teaches us that this [the protection of workers' rights and privileges] only can be accomplished when the men engaged in a certain industry are organized under one single head." Though the Brotherhood learned that lesson early, it was a costly one and not easily absorbed by others. Fratricide was the price paid by carpenters in city after city as conflict broke out between the Brotherhood and the Amalgamated Society of Carpenters and the Amalgamated Wood Workers. In the 1902 New York City strike, for example, the 604-member Amalgamated Society insisted on fifty percent of all the work, and when the boss carpenters and builders acceded, turning away half of the Brotherhood members, the others walked off the job, saying, "If American bosses prefer to hire and employ foreign mechanics to perform one-half of the work, then they can do it all." It was a hot, sharp fight, lasting over seven weeks. It was also, as Duffy noted, "a fight of the Brotherhood against all other trades . . . or, in other words, a fight of 10,000 of our members against 70,000 men."

At stake in the conflict with the Wood Workers was successful organization of the mill men. While this division lasted, it had a retarding effect on general interests. The contest took years of persistent agitation and was forced to the attention of all organizations affiliated with the American Federation of Labor. Much bitterness was injected into the conflict, and the entire reign of General President Huber was mixed up with this controversy.

At both the Toronto and St. Louis conventions of the A. F. of L., 1909 and 1910 respectively, the Carpenter-Wood Worker controversy consumed a good deal of the time of the delegates. Somewhat exasperated, the Federation finally decided that this country was not large enough to hold two organizations of the one craft. The A. F. of L. Executive Council, in 1912, stated: "Every effort has been made to carry into effect the spirit as well as the letter of the declaration of the Atlanta convention of *one organization for one trade*; that duality and rivalry must cease so far as we have the power to enforce it." And so the Federation learned the lesson so clearly stated by *The Carpenter* some ten years before.

The Amalgamated Wood Workers, which had competed with the Brotherhood for twenty-five years, became a part of the Union three years later; the remaining American branches of the British-based Amalgamated Society were absorbed in 1916. The United Brotherhood of Carpenters and Joiners of America faced the future as "One Organization . . . One Trade."

V

"SECOND TO NONE"

In his first report, on April 7, 1913 to the General Executive Board, General President James Kirby remarked "perhaps at no time in the history of the organization have there been so many requests for the sanction of trade movements and for the assistance of organizers." Kirby also reported difficulty in assigning organizers to organizing work, their time being largely consumed in trade movements and other matters affecting the Brotherhood.

It was indeed a busy time for the bustling Brotherhood. From Pacific Grove, California, to Boston, Massachusetts, requests poured in for sanction of movements for wage increases (50 cents a day in Pacific Grove; five cents an hour in Boston). Terre Haute, Indiana sought strike approval for an increase in wages from forty to fifty cents per hour; Bay City, Michigan, went out for five cents more an hour and a Saturday half holiday. Sheboygan, Wisconsin carpenters wanted approval for a shot at a seven-hour day from November 1 to March 1. Over the two years, 1912-1914, the G.E.B. received 301 requests for sanctions, approving 286 with full financial support—$4 a week then $6 a week after October, 1913— to all members answering strike roll call for a week. From Quebec and Jonquireres, Canada came requests for appropriations for organizing purposes. The G.E.B. allocated $150 and $100, respectively.

James Kirby, a millwright from South Chicago, was admirably suited to the task of sorting out the pressing claims upon the

James Kirby— Thirteenth General President

national organization from the local unions and district councils. Born near Kankakee, Illinois in 1855, he moved to Chicago as a youth where he joined Local Union 199. His first achievement was to bring the Chicago millwrights into the union. He became president of the sometimes contentious Chicago District Council and then president of the Structural Building Trades Alliance and first president of the A. F. of L. Building Trades Department. He succeeded Huber in 1912, and died in office on October 5, 1915.

Frank Duffy at desk.

Under the new law, embodied in constitutional amendments adopted at the 1912 convention, the General Officers were now members of the General Executive Board along with one member from each of the union's seven districts. This facilitated the work of the organization, making for smoother relations and greater efficiency. Beginning with the Huber presidency, there was a greater continuity in leadership at the national level. But it was Frank Duffy, the genial General Secretary, who would truly bridge the generations, having served the labor movement for seventy-five years at the time of his death on July 11, 1955.

Frank Duffy was born on May 6, 1861 in Ireland, the oldest child of Philip and Catherine McArdle Duffy. The Duffys were farmers, having had a home in Drumdreenia; as Duffy placed it in a letter to his sister some ninety years later, "that is east of Carrick McCross on the way to Culloville, which is east of County Monaghan." Philip Duffy lost the farm, having stood bail bond to a friend, who then skipped the country. When Frank was two, his parents moved to Liverpool where the elder Duffy worked to support a growing family, in time seven girls and two boys, later moving to Bolton where various members of the family went to work in the cotton mills. "I passed all the grades in the public schools," Frank Duffy wrote his sister, "but yet I was not satisfied. I wanted to secure a higher education," which he did by attending Bolton Mechanics Evening Institute for several years studying the higher branches—Euclid, algebra, square root and cube root, practical, plain and solid geometry, model shading and free hand, physical geography, etc.

Though Duffy walked away with the Queen's prize, top honors, in three subjects, he was not content. "To my young mind," he wrote his sister, "it appeared that I should go to some other country to live." A brother-in-law in New York City, a thriving boss carpenter, sent for young Frank, who arrived in his early twenties eager for "a better chance" as a fledgeling carpenter. "I worked at the trade from every angle. I was journeyman carpenter for years; foreman for years; superintendent for years and took an active part in all things, especially in the Carpenters Union."

He joined Lodge 2 of the United Order of American Carpenters and Joiners, the leading organization of the craft in the East at the time, and played a key role in amalgamation of the Order and the Brotherhood in 1888. "Back in that age," W. J. Shields wrote in 1904, Duffy "was the same strong, energetic, hustling character that we find him today, and much credit is due him for the aid he personally furnished in bringing the two sides together." Duffy became a member of Local Union 488, serving in every office within the gift of that Local. When the Executive Council of Greater New York was formed in 1899, he was elected its first president and was re-elected for five consecutive terms. He was a delegate to the 1896, 1898 and 1900 conventions, was appointed a general organizer in 1896, but could give only a part of his time because he was also serving as a business agent. He was nominated as a member of the General Executive Board several times, turning down the offer on behalf of friends who wanted the position, finally accepting in 1900.

When General President Huber offered Duffy the General Secretaryship, he refused, saying that he had a good job in New York and did not care to move. He and P. J. McGuire were old friends, and Duffy did not feel right about taking the post. But Huber insisted on submitting his name to the General Executive Board and Duffy was drafted. He served for forty-seven years, retiring as General Secretary Emeritus in 1948. (His wife, Catherine R. Duffy, died in 1949.) He was elected a vice-president of the American Federation of Labor in 1913, and held that position for twenty-six years, declining to run in 1939.

Duffy was a beloved figure, often elected unopposed when others faced tough opposition. As editor of *The Carpenter*, he embellished its pages with a certain literary grace. He was fond of sentimental poetry, in particular the poems of the Irish poet, Tom Moore, and enjoyed the songs of Ireland, above and beyond all others, "Mother Macree." His separation from his family seems to have been something of a break; he did not write home for years, though his memories were fond ones. "I never had any ambition to go back to England," he wrote his sister. "I am an adopted son of America. . . . I am proud of it. . . . I have had three sons and five grandsons and two great grandchildren who served with Uncle Sam in the late wars (he wrote his sister in 1954) and I am proud of them. I would not have them do otherwise. The oldest great grandson lost his life in the Italian Invasion and the youngest one had both legs blown off in an explosion in France and still lives."

Duffy personified the carpenter's pride of craft and self-reliance. "If working conditions are to be regulated by law," Duffy wrote in 1916, "then good-by to freedom of contract between employer and employee. We shall have no say in our hours of labor, nor the wages we receive, not the conditions under which we work, nor the people with whom we work. There will then be no such thing as refusal to work with non-union men, as there will be no need of labor organizations whatever. If such existed they could only be looked upon as mutual admiration societies without backbone."

The Brotherhood needed backbone to contend with the assault against trade unionism then underway. In Quincy, Massachusetts mill and factory owners responded to a Carpenters' demand for an increase in wages to 30 cents an hour for a nine-hour day in the fall of 1912 by importing strikebreakers from Chicago. Fortunately, the workers refused the provocation, the Quincy police arrested the "private detectives" for carrying sling-shots and revolvers, and the strike was successful. In Stockton, California, during the course of a six-month lockout involving some 180 Brotherhood members, "private dicks" burglarized a powder magazine near Berkeley and planted the stolen dynamite in a Stockton lumber yard as the first move in an elaborate "frame." The Merchants, Manufacturers and Employers association also worked up "a hospital list" of twenty prominent trade unionists for hired thugs " to get." Luckily, the chief hired gun was caught, and confessed. The anti-labor crusade, as a consequence, collapsed in Stockton.

But the open-shop movement did not collapse so readily elsewhere, largely because the injunction brought the power of the state to bear against unionization. As a December, 1911 editorial in *The Carpenter* put it: "The issuance of injunctions against labor organizations is an enormous power acquired by the courts on the strength of the Sherman Act, a power which some of our judges are stretching day by day. . . ." The costs of fighting injunctions clearly inhibited union growth. Injunction suits and civil cases, over 1912–1914, cost the Brotherhood $104,278, approximately two-thirds of the amount expended on strike benefits ($162,897) over the same period. Money devoured by legal fees, obviously was money not available for organizing or other union needs. In the event, the General Executive Board allocated, mostly in small amounts to the local unions, $21,503 over 1912–1914 for organizing purposes.

The Clayton Anti-Trust Act, enacted by Congress in 1914, provided a measure of relief. The Brotherhood's fees for injunction suits and civil cases, as an instance, dropped to $69,599 over 1914–1916. Hailed by unionists as Labor's Magna Carta, the Act forbade the use of injunctions in labor disputes unless a court decided that one was necessary to prevent irreparable injury to property. It also laid to rest the doctrine of conspiracy in labor cases, making it clear that Sherman anti-trust legislation was not to be construed as forbidding trade unions. "The labor of a human being," it said, "is not a commodity or article of commerce."

But the Act's provisions were soon weakened by court interpretations. Injunction costs once again mounted. Brotherhood General Treasurer Thomas A. Neale reported at the 20th Convention in 1920 that the union had to spend $190,238 defending carpenters against injunctions and civil suits.

Most of the injunctions issued against the Brotherhood were against "restraint of trade" and were aimed at destroying the effectiveness of the Brotherhood's union label, especially in organizing mills making trim. "Few have realized the magnitude of the non-union mill forces that have been marshaled against us," *The Carpenter* commented in a 1914 account of the crucial Paine Lumber case. Emissaries of the American Anti-Boycott Association had been sent out chiefly through the West to awaken the non-union clans, for sympathy and sinews of war, and to get large non-union mills to join together as complainants in the case against the Carpenters.

Eight firms, doing over $8-million worth of business annually and employing over 6,000 men, women and children, applied for injunction in 1911, complaining that the carpenters in New York City had secured such control of the trade that no non-union mill work could be installed in the Borough of Manhattan.* With the

---

* The eight companies were the Paine Lumber Company of Oshkosh, Wis., the W. D. Crooks and Sons Company of Williamsport, Pa., the Gould Manufacturing Company of Oshkosh, Wis., the Bristol Door and Lumber Company of Bristol, Va., the R. McMillen Company of Oshkosh, Wis., the Curtis & Yale Company of Wausau, Wis., Morgan and Company of Oshkosh, Wis., and the Lothman Cypress Company.

$110,000 money chest of the American Anti-Boycott Association at their disposal and attorney Daniel Davenport† to plan their strategy, the eight firms charged a conspiracy to violate the interstate commerce law of the United States and the penal laws of the State of New York. The court was asked to prohibit the Brotherhood: From circulating an "unfair" list; From striking against use of manufactured trim by the eight firms; From carrying out an agreement with the Manufacturing Woodworkers' Association which provided that only Brotherhood members would be employed in the mills, and that outside members would only install union labelled trim; and that members would refuse to install non-union or prison-made material; From ever printing, publishing, or circulating Section 232 of the Brotherhood Constitution, which provides: "It is the duty of all District Councils and Local Unions to promote the use of union-made trim, and to prevent and discourage the use of non-union trim, by refusing to handle same."

The Brotherhood fought back. The stakes were high. Carpenters would in effect be driven to work by court order to undo their fellow members in mills. Paine Lumber was a dominating influence on the non-union mill industry. The character of that industry comes out in the description of Paine's operations given by the union: "That when running in full force it employes about thirty-four hundred men and boys, and about two hundred and fifty women and girls, many of them young boys and girls . . . it is now

† Daniel Davenport was a Connecticut attorney who founded the American Anti-Boycott Association. According to Elias Lieberman, author of *Unions Before the Bar*, he developed the theory behind the infamous Danbury Hatters case, which found the boycott activities of unions illegal under the anti-trust laws *and* held workers *individually* responsible for damages. Anti-union attorneys in the Paine case were also involved in the Bucks' stove case, in which A. F. of L. President Samuel Gompers was indicted because he wrote an editorial in *The Federationist* protesting the injunction that forced him to take the stove company's name off the Federation's "We Don't Patronize" list. As a consequence of the Hatters and Bucks cases the list was discontinued. Workers also became wary of joining unions for fear of being sued. The Supreme Court, in 1915, upheld the right of Dietrich Loewe and Company, the Danbury hat firm, to sue the individual members of the Hatters union for actions undertaken by their officers and confirmed a $252,130.90 judgment against them.

employing one hundred females, of whom fourteen are girls under sixteen years of age; four women who work on circular saws, and ten women employed on glue machinery earning from 9 to ten cents an hour; with work of ten hours a day; that said employment is extremely dangerous. That these wages, and the wages of men running from 12½ to 20 cents an hour in some departments, and 15 to 17 cents in others, are meagre and insufficient." In union mills, women and girls were not employed in the manufacture of wood products. Wages were higher, too, at an averge across the country and in Canada of 42 cents an hour for an eight-hour day. To grant the injunction, the Brotherhood informed the court, would tend to open all mills to women and children at low wages, and destroy the business of about 189 union mills in the city of New York alone, where fair and union wages were paid to men for eight hours' work per day.

The union's counterattack, however, was not limited to the Paine case. When the Anderson and Lind Manufacturing Company of Chicago obtained an injunction in 1913 barring the Brotherhood from enforcing union trim provisions in its contract with Chicago contractors and union mills, the union, after a year-long struggle, succeeded in dissolving the injunction. It then promptly filed suit for recovery of $350,000 in damages. The suit was a much-needed lesson to future injunction seekers.

The Brotherhood also patiently collected evidence of the questionable methods used by the Anti-Boycott Association. It showed that the Association operated a "blind pool" to fight labor, the legal expenses of all cases being borne by the Association. It also showed that the Association was directed by a clique, deciding what action to bring and what money to spend without consulting its members. As a consequence, the New York City district attorney brought criminal prosecutions against three officers of the Association, charging them with practicing law illegally, a violation of the State's penal law which prohibits an association from furnishing lawyers and legal advice to litigants free of charge.

Injunctions alone, of course, are not sufficient to compel men to work against their will, a form of involuntary servitude. It takes an order of a judge to enforce them by declaring somebody in contempt of court. In 1912, in a key case, contempt proceedings were begun in Brooklyn against John Rice, a Brotherhood organizer, for violating an injunction secured by Louis Bossert & Sons. Much to the consternation of the anti-boycott forces, Judge Crane refused to imprison Rice. His decision blazed the way for others favorable to the union. And in June 1917, the United States Supreme Court decided the Paine case in favor of the Brotherhood. It did so, however, on narrow grounds—that under the Sherman Anti-Trust Act a private party could not sue for injunction. The remedy was to apply to the Attorney General and have him institute a suit for injunction. The individual could sue to recover damages as in the Danbury Hatters' case. Unfortunately, the Court majority did not agree with Justice Holmes, who stated that the spirit of the Clayton Act was against such injunctions as sought in the Paine case.

Nonetheless, the Paine decision was a victory for organized labor. As Brotherhood attorney Joseph O. Carson explained, the Court "says you cannot divorce the mill man from the carpenter and say the carpenters shall receive no benefits from helping their fellow members in the mills. They are all one organization and they have a right to act in unity and concert to assist one another, and as long as they do this without malice, then they are not liable." The Court held that the union could not be enjoined as long as the Brotherhood refused as a body to handle any trim or material of a class not organized under the laws of the Brotherhood. "Certainly," said the majority decision, "the conduct complained of has no tendency to produce a monopoly of manufacture or building, since the more successful it is the more competitors are introduced into the trade."

"The decision," *The Carpenter* declared, "should provide impetus to the work of popularizing union mill products and should further encourage us in our efforts to promote the U. B. label on all union trim and union mill work generally."

Promoting the union label meant growth for the Brotherhood. The union experienced its first great jump in membership in several years in 1912–1913, over 23,000 new members that season. After a loss of some 18,000 in the difficult times of 1914 and 1915, it recouped, gaining thousands each year to rise from 194,022 in 1914–1915 to 371,908 in 1919–1920.

On every side there were to be found carpenters, millmen, furniture workers, who by a little persuasion and a little well-meaning pressure could be brought to see that their economic salvation as wage-earners depended upon the success of the labor movement and that by remaining outside its ranks they were injuring themselves as well as their fellow workers.

In July, 1916 Local Union 7 of Minneapolis was praised by *The Carpenter* for its enterprise and energy for recruiting 520 new members in one month, at no cost to the Brotherhood. A splendid spirit of harmony and cooperation enabled the Local to become the largest in the country with 1,909 members and helped, too, in the organization of one of the largest fixture factories in the Northwest.

"The Brotherhood, the country over," *The Cleveland Citizen* remarked in the summer of 1916, "has become a great power.* A carpenter without a union card has a hard row to hoe nowadays if he becomes a traveling journeyman. Wherever he goes he is confronted by a challenge to show his credentials—to prove that he has assisted to improve the working conditions of the men in the craft. If he is unable to prove his worth and good faith he receives little satisfaction.

"And that condition is right and just. The carpenter receives nothing that he does not struggle for, and those who haven't got the courage and manliness to make a fight for better conditions, but who prefer to play the sponge and expect others to wage their battles are not of very much account."†

* In Canada, too, the Brotherhood was prominent. Second in membership, 9,535, to the Railroad Trainmen, 10,401, it became the largest Canadian union with the absorption of 74,116 from the Amalgamated Society in 1914. Tom Moore, born in Leeds, England, in 1879, who joined the Brotherhood in 1909 in Niagara Falls, and, subsequently, moved to Ottawa, became President of the Canadian Trades and Labor Congress in 1917, a post he held for twenty-five years. He died in July, 1946.

† Clearance cards were essential to the discipline of the Brotherhood. No local union, except in the case of a strike or lockout, could reject a legitimate card.

In the course of rapid growth, new challenges emerged for the union and old problems acquired new dimensions. Convention debates, for example, over the election or appointment of organizers reflected the on-going discussion as to how best structure the union democratically and for greater effectiveness. The rank-and-file, some delegates argued, wanted more direct control of the organizers. Another delegate phrased his support of the election of organizers: "The power comes from the great rank and file, they should be the ones to choose their organizers." But the majority considered the election of national organizers impractical. Local, District and State Councils had—still have—the right to nominate, elect and pay their own organizers. The General President, who held the power to appoint organizers under the Brotherhood's constitution, in the words of Delegate Neal was "in the position of the man at the top of the hill who overlooks the surrounding country—he overlooks the entire jurisdiction of the Brotherhood of Carpenters. While we say that local autonomy is all right and many of us insist upon it, still we are out to accomplish the greatest good for the greatest number, and oftentimes it is absolutely essential for one district to sacrifice itself to the interests of a greater number, and we place a man as commander-in-chief of this organization to determine just exactly what shall be done."

"So far as I personally am concerned," President Kirby informed the delegates at the 1914 convention, "the election of organizers will relieve me of a lot of embarrassment. I can simply say, 'Go to your district, and if elected I will consider your appointment and appoint you.' How much easier and nicer it would be to be relieved

---

One source of continual complaint among the locals in certain places was the failure of traveling members to deposit their clearance cards when entering a new locality. Many of these men, particularly when coming into a partially organized region or into the territory of a local paying smaller benefits than the one to which they formerly belonged, retained their cards and even, on request, refused to deposit them. Quite a few of them, it was also charged, often worked longer and at a lower rate of wages than their brothers in that vicinity. This practice almost deserved the name of scabbing. Officers and members were exhorted to stamp out the practice.

from the responsibility that is entailed in the appointment of these men. But it will not get results."

Carpenters had to resolve somehow the tension between local autonomy and the need for a strong central organization. During the latter part of the Huber presidency, and for most of Kirby's term, there was an acrimonious contest for authority between the G.E.B. and the General officers. An obscure hassle over the handling of office supplies occupied much of the officers' and board's time in 1910–1911. As Duffy wrote on February 13, 1911 to his friend, A. F. of L. secretary Frank Morrison, "To tell you the truth we have had a strenuous time." The Brotherhood elections, he added, "were something that I am ashamed of. Scurrilous, defamatory letters went the rounds of our organization. . . . What with the Socialistic element on our Board and the chairman of said board [William G. Schardt] running for General President against Brother Huber, you can readily realize what sort of time we had." After the installation of new officers, friendliness and harmony again prevailed.

Behind the struggles for power and the clash of personalities was a development towards structural reform, one that would integrate successfully the strained relationship between the G.E.B. and the General Officers. Constitutional reforms assigned a greater measure of authority to the General President. The responsibility of the General Officers for the administration of the Brotherhood was clarified as was the responsibility of the President over organizing. The General President was granted constitutional authority to suspend those locals or district councils which either willfully or directly violated the Constitution, laws or principles of the Brotherhood with the consent of the General Executive Board. He could also under new constitutional provisions merge two or more local unions and enforce consolidation provided such course received the sanction of the General Executive Board. As more and more contractors were becoming regional or even national firms, the 1916 convention granted the General President greater supervision of trade movements, i.e., strikes and lockouts, as such movements would involve the members in districts other than the one directly affected. No trade movement, under the new law, was to become effective until such time as the General President had been notified and given an opportunity to make an effort, either in person or by representative, to bring about an adjustment of the controversy.

Carpenters were building a union that could survive the stresses and strains of the Twentieth Century.

VI

A NEW ERA FOR THE BROTHERHOOD

On October 8, 1915 General President Kirby died of a ruptured appendix. He was succeeded by the first general vice-president, William Levi Hutcheson, and the Brotherhood entered a new era.

"Big Bill" Hutcheson was a large man in all senses of that descriptive phrase. Handsome, with lively brown eyes in a strongly moulded face, he carried his 220 pounds on a six-feet-and-one-and-a-half-inch frame with a remarkable grace, exhibiting a like surefootedness in all the major union battles of his time. He was tough-minded, not only over the jurisdictional claims of his fellow carpenters—"Once wood," he liked to say, "it is always the right of the carpenter to install it, no matter what the new material is"—but also when it came to the essential dignity of the working man. "It is not radical," he once said, "to demand that the rights of man should go hand in hand with the rights of property. This is Americanism as I understand it."

Born on January 7, 1874, the eldest boy, third of five (two girls, three boys) children of a Scotch-Irish ship caulker, Daniel Orrich Hutcheson, and his Pennsylvania Dutch wife, Elizabeth Culver, young Bill grew up in Bay County, Michigan, where magnificent stands of white pine still dominated the forests and farms marched behind the advancing lumberjacks. When he was a boy, his father made $2 a day for 12 hours of work. He had little formal schooling, much of that got in the fall, after the potatoes were dug on his father's farm, by walking a mile and a half each way to a country school house. He had to pass through a settlement of German Lutheran immigrants, whose children lay in wait for him. "I learned that it is better to fight than to turn tail," he later said, "and I've never forgotten it."

Young Bill went to work at age 14, helping to erect barns, carpentering in the mines, and working on whatever he could find in the rural areas outside Bay City and Saginaw. At nineteen, he married Bessie King, who became mother of his son, Maurice, another boy (who died in childhood), and two daughters. They were divorced in 1928. He then married Jessie Tufts Sharon, who met her future husband on a train coming east from California, where her ancestors had settled before the Gold Rush. As enterprising youngsters will do, he hunted work wherever he could find it, ranging from Michigan to the Dakota wheatfields to the Idaho forests. He witnessed twenty companies of militia and 250 "Pinkertons" breaking up a strike of lumberjacks and mill-workers in the Coeur D'Alene forests of Idaho.

By 1904, Big Bill landed in Midland, Michigan, working as a carpenter at the Dow Chemical plant. What he saw there he did not much like—wages at 17½ cents an hour for semi-skilled workers, 20 cents, for artisans and 12½ cents an hour for common laborers, including boys and girls. There were plenty of grievances, and when Hutcheson raised some with management on behalf of his fellow workers, he was fired, along with two of his close associates; and he was blacklisted. So he left Midland for Saginaw, where he soon had a job as business agent for Carpenter's Local Union 334 at $16.80 a week. Covering his territory on a bicycle, he must have cut an awkward figure pedalling the union message. His wife kept the books for him, since he also served as local treasurer. In a year, however, he was doing well enough at recruiting new members for the Local to allow enough expense money for the use of a horse and buggy. And, a year later, the Local had grown from a weak union with barely one hundred members to become a model for Southern Michigan, with a loyal membership of 300.

Impressed by his dedication, his fellow carpenters elected him a delegate to the Brotherhood's 1910 convention. Saginaw's carpenters were now working eight hours at $3.20 a day with the right to four legal holidays a year with pay. At the convention, Hutcheson accepted the nomination for the General Executive Board from the Third District. But he lost in what must be one of the Brotherhood's most unusual elections. That year saw the height of the Huber-Executive Board confrontation. According to Wesley C. Hall, who submitted a minority report on the election, Thomas P. Ryan, the chairman of the Committee on the Compilation of Vote for General Officers, was doing his best to take votes from Huber. Nonetheless, both the majority report and the minority gave the election, not only to Huber, but agreed on all the other victors but one—William L. Hutcheson! According to Hall, Hutcheson won handily over a field of seven candidates. (The largest number in any one district, incidentally.) But the majority report gave the Third District post to John H. Potts, who replaced William Schardt, Huber's challenger. Potts served in that position for a good number of years thereafter. Saginaw's Tri-County District Council challenged the count on Hutcheson's behalf (Hall apparently was only interested in the Huber contest), but the G.E.B. denied the request for a recount "as the law does not give the G.E.B. power to order a recount."

Two years later, Big Bill was nominated and elected second vice-president. A year later, Arthur Quinn, the first vice-president stepped down, exchanging places with Hutcheson, as it were, because he wished to remain in New Jersey where he had political interests rather than move to Indianapolis, as a recently passed referendum required. Two years later, President Kirby died and the Saginaw carpenter succeeded to the post. In 1916, he was elected in his own right as General President of the Brotherhood.

Hutcheson had a shrewd grasp of trade union fundamentals. As he once phrased his outlook:

> So, my Brothers, how necessary it should appear to us to prepare as an Organization:
> To resist decreases in wages; to resist increases in hours; to resist encroachments on our jurisdiction.

And we should be further prepared:

To fully and adequately insist on increases in wages; to insist on decreases in hours; to maintain and fully protect all our claims of jurisdiction.

Only through and by solidified ranks, singleness of purpose and a prepared organization, can we hope to wipe out and mitigate injustices, or secure the ends we seek.

So then let us go forth prepared to speak and preach the gospel of a strong militant organization which enforces its laws, which maintains those made by referendum vote, which believes in the keeping inviolate of all agreements made in accordance with those laws, and which believes in such organization, not only for the purpose of aggressiveness, but for the purpose of defense as well!

Jurisdictional conflicts continued to plague carpenters, especially over metal trim and millwrights with the Sheet Metal Workers and the Machinists, as the Brotherhood's stormy relationship with the A. F. of L. Building Trades Department attests. As a carpenter delegate to a Department convention in 1912 put it, "We want a little protection that is all. . . . In city after city, a half dozen trades that would not form one-third party [of our craft] . . . could put our men out of work." In 1914, the membership in referendum voted 40,792 to 13,328 to withdraw from the A. F. of L. Building Trades Department. A testy Sam Gompers reminded the Brotherhood that the Building Trades Department had been founded at the request and general insistence of the United Brotherhood of Carpenters and Joiners. He appeared at the Brotherhood's 1914 convention to express his regret at the withdrawal, saying "that it was, if not a wrong—I shall not accuse you of committing a wrong—I believe it was a mistake: It was a tactical mistake."

When the Building Trades Department called for the expulsion of the Carpenters from the Federation shortly after the Brotherhood's withdrawal, Gompers forestalled the move by a request that the Carpenters return and that the Department reinstate them. By 1915, the Brotherhood was back in, though not without a fight with the Machinists, Iron Workers and Sheet Metal Workers, and not without significant concessions that afforded the Carpenters fair representation within the Department. The Machinists carried their fight to the A. F. of L. 1915 convention, but their resolution calling for the expulsion of the Carpenters failed after a bitter floor fight.

The gravest challenge faced by the Brotherhood in this period, however, came from within, not without, and developed out of a bitter controversy between the national organization and the New York District Council. It had to do with reaching a fruitful balance between local rights and national responsibilities. What started as an economic issue ended as a matter of trade union discipline.

At the start of the 1916 spring season, New York City carpenters had gone nine years without a pay raise. Depressed conditions accounted for this, in large measure, but internal bickering and an inept leadership did not help. Eight thousand unorganized carpenters floating from borough to borough sapped the strength of the union, depressing wages further. In 1914, the Brotherhood's General Executive Board had to deny sanction to a New York strike request, owing to the lack of thorough organization, the large number of men out of work and the fact that fifty-one percent of the members involved (about 40 percent had voted) did not vote in favor of the demand.

Building activity picked up sharply in 1916, and New York carpenters believed that they were in a good position to secure a hefty wage boost in the spring. In January, Elbridge Neal, secretary of the New York District Council, appeared before the G.E.B. to request sanction for a trade movement to secure a 50-cent-a-day increase. The Board consented, agreeing to give financial aid, providing that the New Yorkers undertake an organization drive and build up a strike fund. Negotiations soon bogged down over a 30-cent offer with the employers insisting on an October 1 date, and the union on August 1, for it to take effect. The powerful Building Trades Employers Association remained firm, holding that the unions knew full well that, unlike the lumpers (piecework subcontractors), they were right in the middle of big construction jobs which were undertaken by them under the old wage rates.

The G.E.B. reviewed the New York situation at its April meeting, deciding to invoke the new constitutional provisions, informing the New York carpenters that if an agreement could not be reached before May 1st, the members must not be called out on strike until the General President had an opportunity, through a representative, to bring about a settlement.

The G.E.B. instructions, sent on April 20, were not read to the New York District Council until May 8. On May 1, the New York City carpenters turned out on the call of their business agents. The independent contractors and lumpers capitulated quickly, but the victory was seriously flawed. It was contingent upon scales ultimately settled with the powerful Employers' Association. Moreover, many of the bosses who so promptly signed up on the trade demand for $5.60 a day continued to employ a class of carpenters who were willing to work for any price, from $2.50 per day up.

Hutcheson arrived in New York City on May 5. With Board member Guerin and Vice President Cosgrove, he met with the officers of the District Council, who admitted that the best offer they could get from the Employers' Association was one-half of the 50-cent increase and that they were helpless if it came to a fight to protect and maintain the Brotherhood's jurisdiction. The three general officers met with the Association's negotiation committee and, after considerable discussion, reached a settlement of 50 cents a day, half due on July 1 and half on September 1, 1916.

Hutcheson announced the settlement at a hastily called membership meeting on May 5 where, because of the short notice, only 800 were present. The Distict Council leaders rejected the settlement, whooping up their opposition at a mass protest meeting several days later. On May 12, Hutcheson reported to the General Executive Board and was instructed, by a unanimous vote, to persuade the rebels to accept the agreement negotiated with the Employers' Association and, failing that, to invoke his powers of suspension. Sixty-one of New York's 63 local unions were suspended, and New York carpenters were informed that they could transfer their membership to the non-suspended locals in order to retain their standing and benefits in the Brotherhood.

Then the rebels made a move that lost them whatever sympathy they may have engendered within the Brotherhood over autonomy versus central authority. They hired the noted socialist attorney Morris Hillquit to secure an injunction against the union and its national officers. Hillquit's role raises the question of socialist influence among the New York carpenters and within the Brotherhood. His activity, those loyal to the national administration charged, made it plain as to what element was in the saddle in New York District affairs and who were reaching out for control of the national organization. The Wobblies also got a share of the blame for the chaotic character of the New York situation. The New York leaders, however, were not all socialists, nor, in all likelihood, were most of the members. Hillquit was a prominent labor attorney, sufficient grounds for his retention by the rebels. Nonetheless, socialists had at least one major local and the socialist press supported the New York rebels.

"To my knowledge," Hutcheson told the delegates to the 1916 convention, "such a condition as has been created in New York has never been paralleled in the history of the organization, as the former District Council saw fit TO GO INTO THE CIVIL COURTS AND ASK FOR AN INJUNCTION TO RESTRAIN THE U. B. FROM ENFORCING THE LAWS OF THE ORGANIZATION THAT WERE MADE BY A REFERENDUM VOTE OF THE ENTIRE MEMBERSHIP." (Capitals in the original.) The Committee appointed by the delegates to investigate the New York situation held the injunction more injurious than the breach of discipline on the part of the New York locals. It upheld the suspension and recommended that the 63 New York locals with 17,000 members be re-chartered in consolidated locals with outside men and millmen affiliating with unions known as Millmens' Unions in number not to exceed 25 local unions. A new District Council was ordered. Benefits were to be resumed and continued uninterrupted after a proper financial settlement had been made by the suspended local unions.

Board member Guerin, who was assigned to carry out the task of re-organization, tells what happened: "We boiled the Local Unions down to twenty and districted the city of New York into twenty districts, residence districts, and transferred the individual members to these Local Unions. I appointed temporary officers until such time as all the men were enrolled. We kept the books open for a full six months, giving every man a chance to protect his membership in the organization." The difficult task was carried out so smoothly that only 67 men out of some 17,000 affected requested an adjustment in transfer. Alex Kelso, one of the rebel leaders, subsequently informed the 1920 convention: "We were so far solidified in 1918 that we were able to give the Employers' Association a fight and a lockout . . . with the result that I believe now we are in as good a position in New York City as any city under the jurisdiction of our organization. We are at the present time receiving $9 a day, and I am frank to say that I believe it will be $10 a day on the first of January."

World War I further tested the newly developed strength of the Brotherhood. When war first loomed on distant horizons, the Carpenters along with many other American trade unionists, greeted it with dismay.

When the United States was drawn into the conflict, however, carpenters acted promptly to support their country. Nearly 9,000 served in the armed forces of the United States and Canada; five hundred went to France to work for the Army; and 50,000 worked at home, in shipyards, aviation fields and cantonments. As individual carpenters enlisted in the armed forces, the membership, in referendum, guaranteed that they would not lose their benefits or right of membership. "Our organization consists of patriotic American citizens," a G.E.B. resolution stated, "ready and willing at all times to do their duty when called upon." It backed up sentiment with a concrete offer of help: "If the government officials will only let us know in reasonable time when men are required for industrial service at any particular point designated by the government, we will co-operate with these officials in supplying the men required." When a live-wire Bronx business agent, David Lang, sold $150,000 worth of Liberty Bonds, *The Carpenter* praised his action as typical of the "win-the-war" spirit which characterized all members. Carpenters purchased over $12-million in Liberty Bonds and war savings stamps.

Labor's participation was, of course, crucial to the successful prosecution of the war. America's wartime policy also flowed out of the reforms of the Progressive era, which laid the ground work for an active government role in the economy. President Woodrow Wilson appointed a trade unionist, a former secretary-treasurer of the United Mine Workers, William B. Wilson, as Secretary of Labor. The new Secretary established the Federal Mediation and Conciliation Service, a sign of a more open attitude on the part of government towards organized labor. During the war, for the first time, labor was represented in a host of public agencies, from the Advisory Council of National Defense to fuel, food, emergency construction and war industries boards. At the end of the war, labor was encouraged to send a delegation to the Peace Conference. Brotherhood General Secretary Frank Duffy was a prominent member of the group appointed by the A. F. of L. and headed by A. F. of L. President Samuel Gompers. *

At the A. F. of L. 1917 convention in Buffalo, President Wilson, the first President to so appear, urged a wartime no-strike policy. "Nobody has a right to stop the processes of labor until the methods of conciliation and settlement have been exhausted." He also stressed his wartime policy. "We must," he said, "do what we have declared our purpose to do, see that the conditions of labor are not rendered more onerous by war, but also that we shall see to it that the instrumentalities by which the conditions of labor are improved are not blocked or checked."

Earlier, in June, Secretary of War, Newton D. Baker and A. F. of L. President Gompers had worked out a plan for adjusting "misunderstandings" in war work, including a tri-partite United States Adjustment Commission with one member named by labor. It was agreed that local union rates would be paid for construction work and repairs on cantonments. The A. F. of L. was then informed that the "Government cannot commit itself in any way to the closed shop. . . . The word 'conditions' is, of course, clearly understood to refer only to the arrangement in the event of overtime, holiday work and matters of that kind." Gompers agreed that that was indeed the case.

Brotherhood President Hutcheson took strong exception to this, especially as it was applied to a memorandum involving shipbuilding. As he wrote Gompers:

* The other members were James Duncan of the Granite Cutters, William Green of the Mine Workers, and John R. Alpine of the Plumbers Union.

"There was quite a feeling among our membership that [this] was the opportune time to advance their wage and it was no easy task on the part of the general officers to restrain them from doing so. And we feel that when firms . . . are given contracts by our Government and permitted to employ non-union men therein, even though they may be paying the wage and working the hours established by our organization, it tends to jeopardize, retard, and even tear down the conditions and standards established. We feel that, in all fairness and justice to our membership as citizens of this country, the Government should take steps to see that only contractors that comply with the standards and conditions as established be given governmental contracts."

The government, Hutcheson argued, should avail itself of every instrumentality for the successful prosecution of the war. "Inasmuch as our organization consists of the great majority of the carpenters of the country, the Government should have availed itself of the assistance we would be able to render . . . but we reserve the right as citizens . . . to say whom we would or would not work with . . . so long as there was permitted to exist between us and our Government a profiteer who was paid a percentage on labor performed by our members, . . . if we worked direct for the Government we would raise no question as to whom we worked with."

Shipyards were plagued by unsavory working conditions, and the obdurate United States Shipping Board was of little help. Whenever the Brotherhood offered suggestions for resolving worker grievances, the Board or its labor relations arm, the Shipbuilding Wage Adjustment Board, in effect said "nothing doing." Private contractors, the New York weekly, *The Public*, reported in February, 1918, "have been left free to hire and discharge men as they saw fit and to pay them whatever wages they pleased. A carpenter might leave his home and go to a distant shipyard where housing and working conditions were bad, and where the chaos that characterizes any new construction job begun in a hurry made the work difficult and trying. In many instances he was put to work at common labor, in other instances he was forced to accept employment at his trade at wages less than those prevailing in the district. If a foreman discharged him, whether with prejudice or without, he found himself out his railroad fare and his pains. In some instances large numbers of skilled men answered the Government's call only to find that there was no work ready for them. Worst of all, no uniform consistent policy prevailed. At one shipyard the California applicants for work learned that they must first pledge themselves to buy sandlots on the installment plan from land-owners in league with the shipbuilding company. At another yard applicants were examined as to their membership in a union and if union men they were told they must first tear up their cards."

Hutcheson went to Washington, seeking in vain a meeting with Edward N. Hurley, shipyard owner and head of the Shipping Board. Conference after conference, Secretary Duffy remarked, produced no satisfactory results. The Brotherhood refused to become a party to an open shop agreement. The men wanted to know what was happening. The General President had no other alternative than to truthfully tell them. They waited no longer; they immediately put down their tools and quit.

The walkout on February 11, 1918 affected shipyards in Staten Island and Baltimore. Hurley threw angry imprecations, endlessly repeated in the popular press: "Do you realize that you are adding to the fearful danger our soldiers already face, the danger of starvation and the danger of slaughter if food and ammunition are not sent over in ships and many ships at once? Do you think the fathers and mothers whose sons are making this sacrifice will sit patiently by and permit this paralyzing of the lifeline between us and the western front to go on?"

Frustrated, Hutcheson appealed to President Wilson, but he declined to act, urging that the union abide by the decisions of the Shipbuilding Wage Adjustment Board. Believing that he had no other recourse and that he had exhausted all avenues, Hutcheson complied with the President's request that he urge the men to return to the building of ships. The Brotherhood continued its efforts to reach some fair and equitable agreement with the United States Shipping Board. A wage increase was granted several months later, but the open shop question was never satisfactorily resolved, even after meetings with a young assistant secretary of the Navy, Franklin

D. Roosevelt. In 1920, Hutcheson said, "we were never able to get the War Department or the United States Shipping Board officials to recognize the union conditions established by our membership." But neither did the union ever sign the open-shop agreement.

Hutcheson's objections to the anti-labor elements in the government's labor policy, however, were recognized in the formation of the War Labor Board in 1918, with five labor, five employer and two public members. On the whole, observed Philip Taft, the Board's activities met with the approval of the A. F. of L. The influence of former President William H. Taft, who served on the Board with Hutcheson and became his close friend, was helpful in averting serious stoppages. But, most important was the Board's recognition of the rights of labor to organize and to bargain collectively through representatives of its own choosing. As Hutcheson observed after the war, the work accomplished by that body was a great benefit not only to members of the organization but to workers of the country, because the records would show that in the cases that were brought before the Board for consideration, fair and impartial hearings were given and that the findings made in the majority of cases were favorable to workers.

Hutcheson summed up the Brotherhood's experience at the 1920 convention: "Inasmuch as Organized Labor is an institution or organization of mechanics, the Government should have given them the same consideration and recognition as was given associations of financial interests and manufacturing establishments. Since this was not done, it was therefore necessary that constant attention be given to matters affecting our membership in order to maintain the standards we had established and to retain unto ourselves the rights, benefits and priviliges guaranteed to us under the laws of our country."

The Brotherhood's concerns during the difficult war years not only embraced the task of winning the war but also that of establishing the peace to follow. Reconstruction, the Brotherhood recognized, was essential to the economic well-being of the country as it recovered from the wounds of war. To give the country a much needed immediate lift, it urged that all building construction "retarded by reason of the war" be put into operation. It warned against wage reductions, urged equal pay for equal work, irrespective of sex, promoted a due regard for ability to make provision for old age, and urged the establishment of state and national employment offices. Veterans were to be assured their old jobs; public works were devised to allay depression during the transition from war to peace; the National War Labor Board continued. The Brotherhood also advocated the franchise for women, the establishment of a World Trade Union Congress and it endorsed President Wilson's proposal for a League of Nations.

"What will be the thoughts of those coming back," *The Carpenter* asked in an April, 1919 editorial, "who at their country's call to arms gave heed and went away over 3,000 miles, to what to them was an unknown country, to fight the great cause for democracy and freedom, leaving their homes and loved ones, their work and opportunities, and after fighting and suffering to sustain the great cause for which they risked their all, to come back and face the dread spectre of unemployment and again renew the fight in their own country, to win back what they are justly and rightfully entitled to, the work they left unfinished."

What indeed?

VII

THE AMERICAN PLAN

On November 29, 1919, four members of the Brotherhood—
Lum E. Williams, Thomas Gaines, H. J. Bouchillon and S. J.
O'Rourke—were shot down in broad daylight as they emerged from
the offices of the Central Labor Union in Bogalusa, Louisiana.
They were murdered because they dared organize their fellow black
and white workers at the Great Southern Lumber Company. It was
an ominous opening for the decade ahead.

At the end of World War I, the Brotherhood was optimistic.
Peace would bring prosperity, renewed building and growth for the
union. As Frank Duffy put it in his first 1920s editorial, "It would
be a splendid thing for the United Brotherhood if every one of its
345,000 members faced the new year with a firm determination to
do something tangible for it within the next twelve months and
assist in so far as they are able in bringing the organization up to
the 500,000 mark in that space of time."

But the Brotherhood's hopes for a half-million membership
ran head-long into a stiffened employer opposition, a renewed drive
for the open shop embodied in the so-called American Plan.

The steel industry, in 1919, successfully smashed a valiant
organizing drive mounted by the American Federation of Labor.
Encouraged, employers took advantage of a patriotism enhanced
by war and victory and linked their anti-union drive to Americanism.
"The open shop," they said, would give "equal opportunity to all
and special privileges to none." National Association of Manufac-

turers' president John Edgerton solemnly declared: "I can't conceive of any principle that is more purely American, that comes nearer representing the very essence of all those traditions and institutions that are dearest to us than the open-shop principle."

The open-shop drive was given added impetus by the U. S. Supreme Court 1917 decision in *Hitchman Coal Company* v. *Mitchell*. The Court held that an individual contract not to join a union—what unionists scornfully termed, "the Yellow Dog Contract"—was valid, that inducement to join a union was a breach of contract, and that the right to strike was not a right to instigate a strike. Employers had the weapon they neeeded to combat unionization. Before getting a job, a prospective employee had to sign an agreement that he would not, while employed, join a union or attempt to organize his fellow workers. Strikes where such "contracts" existed became illegal strikes; if continued, they became strikes against government itself. Open shops became closed non-union shops where union members were either discharged or denied employment.

The Carpenters' drive in Bogalusa began the year of the Supreme Court decision. The Great Southern Lumber Company boasted the largest saw mill in the world. When Brotherhood organizer Rodgers arrived in Bogalusa, he was arrested and while in jail, dynamite caps and fuses were planted in his grip. Rodgers, however, was released by Federal authorities, and the carpenters of Bogalusa began their union.

Company thugs took the president of the Sawyers' Local, drove him five miles out of town, and beat him until he wrote a letter to his wife, telling her to sell their small farm and to leave Louisiana at once. Mayor Sullivan, who also happened to be a vice president of Great Southern, placed company henchmen on the Bogalusa police force and they began, in a local carpenter's words, "a reign of terror," arresting union men, both black and white, on trumped up charges.

The president of the Colored Timber Workers' Union owned a home and live-stock valued at about $5,000. He was offered $2,000 for his property and was told to leave town. He refused, and that night his house was shot up. Fortunately, he had informed his white brothers of the bribery attempt and they hid him from the "authorities." The press was told that Lum Williams, president of the Central Trades Council, and another union sympathizer had paraded the Colored Timber Workers' president up and down the street while they were heavily armed and dared the police to arrest them. This gave the authorities the excuse to arrest Williams. Armed with a warrant, they drove up to the union office, shot Williams as he came out the door, and the other three Carpenters were killed as they came out with their hands up. Lum Williams' younger brother then shot the police captain in the shoulder with a 22 calibre rifle. He was arrested immediately and charged with intent to kill. The thirteen murderers in uniform were arraigned by a Grand Jury several weeks later and released on $40,000 bonds. They resumed their police work of intimidation by continually arresting negroes for vagrancy and placing them in the city jail.

The Bogalusa attack was the first of many aimed at the Brotherhood during the 1920s.

At the 1924 Indianapolis convention, President Hutcheson spelled out the triple-threat, "attempts made to disrupt not only the morale of the membership of our organization, but the conditions that have been established." These attempts, Hutcheson said, were made by different forces: *Employers*, backed by the Manufacturers' Associations, the Chamber of Commerce, etc., carrying out the "American Plan"; rival *unionists*, "some of the other building trades organizations attempting to force our membership to accept a condition that is not in conformity with the laws, rules, regulations and jurisdictional claims of our Brotherhood;" *Communists*, "another form of attack . . . more insidious than either of the others . . . [because it] has been made in many instances from within our organization by men who have been misled into believing that the propaganda that has been spread by men like Foster [a founder of the Communist Party in the United States] and his kind was more in keeping with Organized Labor than the principles of our organizations."

Admittedly, the Brotherhood was in good shape to withstand the attacks enumerated by Hutcheson. For carpenters, the 1920s was a building decade. For one thing, total new construction rose for most of the decade; starting at $6-million in 1921, it peaked at $12-million in 1926, held at that in 1927, dropping to $10.7-million in 1929. Significant, too, was a development remarked upon in a 1928 *Carpenter* editorial; "We are glad to note that the old custom of discontinuing building activities during the winter months is gradually going into the discard."

In Canada, conditions were not quite so favorable. However, economic well-being in the building industry of the United States had been beneficial to the men of the trade in some parts of Canada. During the previous four years thousands of organized men left Canada to come across the line. Emigration caused genuine concern, and in some districts of Canada where organization existed in the form of Local Unions of the Brotherhood, a raise in wages was secured.

In the big cities, Chicago, Cleveland, St. Louis, New York, where carpenters were getting $9–12 for an 8-hour day in 1920, they were earning $12–13.50 by the end of the decade. Local Union No. 180, Vallejo, California, reported obtaining the five-day week in July, 1925; it was not alone in the five-day week movement. But the movement did not become general in the 1920s.

Despite a loss of 36,862 "war babies," men who entered the trade in war-time and later left, the Brotherhood held its own in membership, remaining the largest organization of skilled mechanics in the Labor Movement of the continent. Members in good standing numbered better than 325,000 for most of the period, dropping to 300,000 in 1928, and to 283,635 in mid-1929. Total membership—good standing plus those in arrears of 6-months or less—peaked in 1926 at 404,917. This—and a healthy $700,000 surplus in the treasury—enabled the Brotherhood to withstand the anti-union buffeting of the 1920s.

Within the Brotherhood, throughout much of the 1920s, there was a lively debate over pensions and the establishment of a Home for Aged Carpenters. Gabriel Edmonston broached the idea in 1910. President Kirby raised it again in 1914. He reminded convention delegates, "we are growing older day by day, and sooner, perhaps, than we realize, will reach that period in life when we will find that securing employment is an uphill proposition." Most members agreed with Joseph Rieul, West New York, New Jersey Local 612, who wrote to *The Carpenter*: "I joined the union in 1881. That means that for 46 years I have faithfully paid my dues and kept its rules. Now that I am no longer able to compete with the younger men, I do not think it is charity but only justice for the union to help us." Though a few agreed with one crusty old-timer, who wrote in response to a pension proponent, "Why does he expect the younger generation of wood butchers, who have troubles of their own in this age of high living, to dig up for his old age? . . . The brother is looking for something for nothing and that has been to the great detriment of organization. That's the reason why we are not respected. I expect to starve to death in a few more years myself, but am not expecting the younger generation to thwart my expectations in the least."

In truth, however, few carpenters had such a Hobbesian view of the world. In 1923, the members, in referendum, 55,000 to 24,000, voted for the purchase of land for a home for aged and infirm carpenters and authorized a ten-cent-per-capita increase to pay for the home and a pension. But there were delays, inevitable perhaps in a democratic organization. Opponents of the home forced a referendum proposing the sale of the land acquired in Lakeland, Florida, for the home. The referendum was defeated, and the Brotherhood proceeded with construction but found that the ten-cent home/pension levy was insufficient to support both. A referendum to raise 25 cents more a month failed to secure the necessary two-thirds to pass, though a majority voted in favor. As First General Vice-President George H. Lakey put it, the referendum "left us in a position whereby we have a most wonderful Home, and we have a Pension Law, but not enough money to pay a Pension." Another referendum in 1929, however, succeeded. By 1930, 200 old-timers were at the Home and members over 65, of 30 years good standing, who did not care to avail themselves of its facilities, were entitled to a $15-a-month pension.

"Fancy if you can," wrote John J. Leary, Jr., in the *New York World*, "laboring men enjoying the comforts of a first-class city hotel plus an 18-hole golf course, said to be the finest in the South,

Carpenters' Home in Lakeland, Florida.

a private lake to fish in and an orange grove of 1000 acres to ramble through—all without cost to themselves. That, in a nutshell, is what the United Brotherhood of Carpenters and Joiners of America is providing for its superannuated and incapacitated members in the $3,000,000-Home just outside of the city limits of Lakeland, Florida."

With the pick-up in post-World War I building construction, there was general agreement that jurisdictional disputes were a grave handicap. In an effort to do something about this, representatives of the A. F. of L. Building Trades Department met with representatives of the architects, the engineers and the contractors organizations. In June, 1919, a proposed National Board of Jurisdictional Awards in the Buiding Industry was approved by all parties. Though Brotherhood President Hutcheson was named one of the three labor representatives on the Board, the Brotherhood's officers were wary, agreeing, in Hutcheson's words, that "we would be damned if we did [participate] and we would be damned if we didn't." The Board's rules required a two-thirds vote of an eight-man Board, three labor/ five employer members, to enforce an award. Despite the likelihood that the employer side could consistently outvote the unionists, the Brotherhood, reluctantly, decided to go along, provided that certain questions were answered satisfactorily and the action was approved at the Brotherhood's next convention. *

The Brotherhood's reservations—and suspicions—about the Board were soon proved fully warranted. The Board met in November, 1920, to dispose of several disputes involving carpenters. Hutcheson, as the Board's rules provided, asked for a postponement because the Brotherhood's General Executive Board had not received answers to the questions it had posed and, therefore, could not adequately consider participation. Despite this, the Board proceeded, rendering several decisions without hearing the Broth-

---

* The Brotherhood G.E.B. wanted to know: "The manner in which the Board of Jurisdiction Awards was created; its functionings and possible accomplishments; the benefits that would be derived from its make-up; the percentage of contractors affiliated with it; the percentage of architects and engineers, and what they would do to carry out decisions reached."

erhood's side of the case. In particular, it decided that the erection of hollow metal trim should be done by sheet metal workers.

Carpenters were shocked, not only because of the patent unfairness in the handling of the case but also because the controversy over metal trim was, by 1920, a dead issue. Ninety-five percent of it had been done by carpenters because it required the knowledge, skill and training of a carpenter to do that work in a satisfactory and proper manner. A controversy was stimulated, when none in fact existed.

Proponents of the open shop, especially among architects, made the most of the issue. As E. J. Russell, the architects' representative on the Board, declared: "We are going to . . . educate them [union leaders] along the very best lines. . . . We are going to get them to consider the question of grading men as to quality and as to wage and . . . to consider their time limitations as to the work a man shall do. All these things will come." In 1922, the American Institute of Architects endorsed the American Plan. "We have the open shop coming into popularity," said St. Louis architect William B. Ittner, prime mover of the open shop resolution at the Architects' Institute's 1922 convention. "That means . . . that our Board should be instructed [to] see what changes can be made in order to bring the principle [of the Jurisdictional Awards Board] into accord with the sentiment of the Institute."

The open shop wedge was in place; all that remained was for employers to swing the hammer, set union against union. In the fall of 1922, Frank Duffy reported "various building tradesmen refuse to work where members of our organization have been employed in the erection of metal trim and there have been occurrences where they have gone so far as to refuse work on buildings where our men were employed where there was no controversy over the jurisdiction of work."

"The Brotherhood of Carpenters," President Hutcheson told delegates to the 1921 Building Trades Department convention, "are not looking for a fight, but if they have to fight they will fight all the way, and the sooner it is started the sooner it will be over."

Fight back they did, winning the support of the A. F. of L., even though the Brotherhood and the Building Trades Department

*AFL Executive Council, Washington, D.C. Front row, l. to r.—
Dan'l J. Tobin, Sam'l Gompers, Frank Morrison, Matthew Woll.
Back row, l. to r.—T. A. Rickert, Frank Duffy, James Duncan, Jos.
H. Valentine.*

parted company. The Department demanded the suspension of the
Carpenters from the A. F. of L.; the Federation Executive Council
unanimously rejected that proposition, further informing the Building Trades Department that fundamental principles were being
violated by building tradesmen enforcing the awards of the Board

of Awards. Strikes of union workmen against other union workmen were intolerable, the Council declared, urging that such practices should be discontinued.

Slowly but surely, the Building Trades Department came around. There was a change in the leadership, and by 1924, William Tracy of the Plumbers, the new Secretary of the Department, was able to report to A. F. of L. President William Green, "a better feeling exists between the United Brotherhood of Carpenters and Joiners and its officials and our Department than has existed since 1921."

That new feeling was concretely expressed in a new and definitive agreement between the Carpenters and the Sheet Metal Workers. The National Board for Jurisdictional Awards, in effect, was abolished. Building tradesmen praised the idea behind the Board, but at Hutcheson's insistence, declined to join in another such effort until "definite assurances can be given . . . that [employers represented on the Board] severally agree to employ none but Union Building Trades Mechanics throughout."

During the 1920s, the Brotherhood played an increasingly important role within the labor movement and within society-at-large. The Brotherhood joined the International Union of Woodworkers, an international confederation of trade unions with affiliates in fourteen countries with memberships totalling 626,779. When fellow trade unionists were in trouble, carpenters gave aid, and gave it generously. From time to time, the A. F. of L. issued appeals for aid for different purposes. The Brotherhood gave: $1,480 to aid German unionists; $29,747 for the 1926 Anthracite Coal Miners' strike; $12,538 for the 1927 British Miners' strike; $856 for the Ladies Garment Workers' strike of 1927; and $1,469 for the United Textile Workers' strike of the same year.

Though the Brotherhood's constitution excluded party politics from its meetings, carpenters were, inevitably, drawn into the political life of their country. Hutcheson was an active Republican; Duffy, a life-long Democrat, just to give two examples. P. H. McCarthy was elected mayor of San Francisco and, as The Carpenter noted in 1926, "Union carpenters [in California] have been represented in every department of our city government and in our

State Legislature. Their work as public officials has reflected credit upon themselves and their union organization." In Canada, Brotherhood locals were more directly involved in political action. Local 452, Vancouver, for example, endorsed its president, James Reed, as alderman candidate in 1919, and, five years later, became affiliated with the Canadian Labor Party. James F. Marsh, Brotherhood representative in Ontario, became Deputy Minister of Labor for that Province in 1928, a tribute to his contribution in fashioning apprenticeship standards in Canada and to the Brotherhood's standing.

When the A. F. of L. Executive Council considered endorsing Senator Robert M. LaFollette, the Progressive Party's Presidential candidate, the Brotherhood opposed the move. Duffy, then A. F. of L. Second General Vice President, cast the only vote against endorsement. He argued that labor's vote could not be delivered and that trade unions ought not tell the members how to vote. The Brotherhood adhered to its non-partisan policy in 1924, as it has in other years, though carpenters did contribute $923 to the Federation's National Non-Partisan Political Fund on behalf of the LaFollette candidacy.

"We are not striking so much as we did but we are voting more," Joseph Reed, a Madison, Wisconsin, carpenter wrote to *The Carpenter* in 1927, reflecting a growing awareness of the importance of the vote among trade unionists. One reason, certainly, for this was the growing importance of legislation to the labor movement. In the same issue, Alex Kelso, secretary-treasurer of the New York District Council, urged support of legislation that, enacted three years later, became the Davis-Bacon Act. "Contractors," he wrote, "erecting federal buildings cannot bring cheap labor from an outside state and underbid local contractors if [the proposed measure] becomes law."

As workers active in their union and in the political life of their country, carpenters were among the first to oppose Communism. When the Communists seized power in Russia their first moves were the suppression of a freely-elected Constituent Assembly called to draft a democratic constitution after the overthrow of the Czar and the suppression of free trade unions. Taking their lead from the new czars of Russia, the American Bolsheviks in 1919 launched an attack on American trade unions, calling upon workers to organize Councils of Workers, Soldiers and Sailors. Later, they went underground, seeking to penetrate unions by boring from within.

"There is no fraternal or patriotic society today that our members have not the right to join," Brotherhood President Hutcheson declared, but the Communists "mean no good for the bona fide trade body . . . [They] are attempting to stir up class feeling, segregate the union men from their own organization, and cause strife and discord in our ranks."

In truth, the Communist appeal for revolutionary Councils attracted only a few. But, as Vancouver carpenter James Kelly observed in an October 1919 letter to *The Carpenter*: "They appear to have quite a large following of the working people, partly because of their soap-box oratory and partly because of the many abuses and injustices dealt out to the working class by those in power; the power we elect and expect to do our business for us on the square, stand in with the greedy profiteers, while a lot of the members we elect and pay to do our business, forget they are our servants, and abuse the trust we placed in them." Kelly warned his fellow workers against the Communists because, in his experience, "the Bolshevik reign in Vancouver at present . . . is as arbitrary and tyrannical as they put up in Russia."

By the mid-1920s, under the guise of a so-called Trade Union Educational League, the Communists were exploiting beachheads established in two New York City locals and their influence among a scattering of Carpenter locals in several major cities. Their goal was the capture of the Brotherhood or its destruction.

R. C. Wonderberg, the Secretary of the International Union of Woodworkers, a guest at the Brotherhood's 1928 convention, gives a vivid eyewitness account of what happened.

> Much time was taken up by the report of the Committee on Appeals and Grievances . . . The principal case was that of New York Local No. 375, whose charter had been revoked because of their refusal to submit their books for examination to the duly authorized deputy of the General President. The members of the

suspended Local, which was under communist control, had been allowed to go over to other Locals without loss of privileges. . . .The leader of the communist opposition within the Brotherhood, Morris Rosen, was present as a visitor. He was granted the floor to defend the action of his former Local. In the manner known only too well among European trade unionists, too, Rosen abused the privilege granted him by delivering a speech full of defamatory insinuations against the officers of the United Brotherhood, and particularly against President Hutcheson. . . .Such familiar epithets as, 'Czar Hutcheson' and 'servants of the Capitalist class' made me almost feel at home. After Rosen had had his say, General Secretary Duffy got up and stripped bare before his audience the cunningly woven texture of tricks and humbug which serve the communist opposition to carry on propaganda for their baneful aims. . . .

The Convention decided then and there to expel Rosen and several of his friends from the organization. Others . . . were required to sign a declaration to the effect that they were members neither of the Workers' (communist) party of America nor of the Trade Union Educational League, and were placed on probation under the supervision of the General President and their District Council. But two more members were expelled, making a total of seven.*

The Communists were routed from the Brotherhood, though they continued to plague the labor movement until the Communist-controlled unions were expelled from the Congress of Industrial Organization in 1948. The Carpenters' experience was helpful to other unions combatting the same dangers of infiltration and disruption. In the late 1920s, for example, the International Ladies' Garment Workers' sought the Brotherhood's advice in its battle against Communist control and subversion.

---

* The newsletter of the Moscow Red Trade Union International would have its readers believe that the whole New York District Council were under Communist control, and that Morris Rosen had been elected delegate of the New York Carpenters' organization. How to make this tally with the further assertion that the charter of the District Council had been revoked by "Czar" Hutcheson, and a number of members excluded from the Unions, does not greatly concern these past masters in the art of faking reports. It should be noted that the Communists were in control of just one of the over thirty New York Locals, and that Rosen was present at the Convention as a visitor, not as a delegate.

"One should not be deceived as to what the so-called 'American Plan' means," *The Carpenter* editorialized in January, 1921. "It is the re-titling of the scheme of the manufacturers of a decade past who set out to crush the movement of organization among the working men and women of this continent under the banner of the 'open shop.' "

"Capital's declaration of war upon organized labor," the editorial continued, "has come at a most unfortunate time, and will have disastrous consequences, but in the long-run, which may be very soon, the counter-offensive of radical forces which have been recruited by the fatal and futile course of reaction will sweep away the last vestiges of industrial peace and bring about far-reaching economic changes that may not be altogether to the liking of our financial and industrial interests."

The Brotherhood bore the brunt of the attack. Citizen committees sprang up in city after city, town upon town. St. Louis, reported *The Carpenter* in March, 1922, boasted that 68 percent of its privately owned institutions were operating on the open shop plan. That year, the National Association of Manufacturers bragged that 36 percent of all cities were building under open shop conditions. The spread of the Yellow Dog contract, first prominent in the New England textile industry in the 1870s, to coal, hosiery, street-railway, and the shoe industries during the 1920s intensified industrial strife.* Private detective agencies flourished like speak-easies during Prohibition, "the biggest lot of blackmailing thieves that ever went unwhipped," according to detective William J. Burns. One A. F. of L. official estimated that there were 200,000 industrial spies at work in 1928. The annual income of the three leading agencies during the decade was estimated at $65,000,000. The introduction of armed hoods as "finks" (strikebreakers), or as "nobles" (armed guards), facilitated the entry of gangsters into the lucrative business of industrial and craft racketeering.

Trade unions were hard hit. The Machinists, a choice Amer-

---

* *The Carpenter* reproduced a sample Yellow Dog contract in the March, 1922 issue. The laborer who gave the contract to *The Carpenter* exacted "a most solemn pledge" that his name would not be used.

ican Plan target, dropped from 330,800 members in 1920 to 77,900 in 1924. According to Leo Wollman, overall union membership peaked at 5,047,800 in 1920. By 1923, it was down to 3,622,000, falling thereafter to less than three million in 1933. In 1920, union membership constituted 19.4 percent of nonagricultural employees; in 1930, a scant 10.9 percent. The American Plan was not the sole reason for the decline, but it sure helped.

"Thousands of men have been brought to Chicago," Second General Vice President George H. Lakey reported in a classic account of the American Plan in operation, "dumped on the labor market; many of them classed as unfit or unwilling—most all of them unfamiliar with the conditions under which they must labor in a big city."

The flood of unwanted workers was called forth to depress wages. Chicago employers, in the spring of 1921, opened a drive

---

NON UNION AGREEMENT
(NO.)   (DATE)

The undersigned, whose craft is that of a _____

in accepting employment from _____

in its shops in _____ does
so upon the understanding and agreement with said employers:

(1) That, as to said craft, said shop has been operated, and will continue to be operated, upon non-union basis and is non-union.

(2) That said employer will not recognize, nor have any dealings with, any labor union composed of persons engaged in or representing said craft.

(3) That said employe is not a member of any labor union. While employed by said employer, said employe will not become a member of any labor union and will have no dealings, communications or interviews with the officers, agents or members of any labor union in relation to membership by said employe in such labor union, or in relation to said employe's said employment.

(4) That it is the intention and desire of said employer and employe that the employment relation between them be kept entirely free from interference or intervention in any respect by any labor union, its officers or agents.

(Employe's name) _____

(Employe's address) _____

---

to reduce wages to pre-World-War-I levels. They induced the weaker unions to accept "arbitration," and requested that Judge K. M. Landis make an "award"—$1.10 an hour in a $10-a-day town. Then they organized a "Citizens Committee to Enforce the Landis Award."

With the Carpenters taking the lead, the Painters, Plumbers, Sheet Metal Workers, Laborers, Fixture Hangers, Roofers, Hoisting Engineers, Glaziers, Cement Finishers, Terrazzo Workers and Lathers refused to accept the Landis Award. (The Carpenters and several others had had nothing to do with it from the start.) The Citizens Committee spent over a million dollars to enforce the Award.

The Brotherhood fought back. The District Council published 200,000 pamphlets to tell the union's story to the public. On April 29, 1922, over 60,000 carpenters and building tradesmen marched through the streets of the Windy City in protest.

President Hutcheson met with the chief executives of three key national firms—Thompson-Starrett, John Griffiths & Sons Company and the Fuller Construction Company. He minced no words, telling them that they must "at once comply with and conform to the established working conditions of our membership in Chicago, otherwise, we would take steps to remove our members from their work elsewhere."

It was a salutory conversation. The three firms announced that they were through with both the Chicago Citizen's Committee and the Landis Award.

The struggle continued for another six months, but the end was in sight. In June, the Brotherhood negotiated a two-year contract fixing a minimum scale of $1.25 an hour and covering 20,000 carpenters. In August, Frank Duffy announced that for all practical intents and purposes the Landis Award was a dead issue in the building trade in Chicago.

The Brotherhood beat back the American Plan in Seattle, Salt Lake City and Los Angeles, among other leading cities. But the crucial battle took place in San Francisco, where folks were forced into the American Plan by the likes of "Black Jack" Jerome, a hood with a winning way with a sand-filled sock.

The opening for the American Plan in San Francisco was provided, as in Chicago, by an invitation from the Industrial Association to participate in an Impartial Wage Board. In rejecting the offer, the Brotherhood's District Council stated:

> We have never increased our wage scale, except through conferences and by agreement reached with our employers. . . .Our membership roll is never closed, our Locals are open to every qualified carpenter, the negro as well as the white man. We encourage the employment of apprentices, and maintain schools for their instruction. We believe in industrial peace and have worked constantly to maintain it, but we deny the right of any man or men to determine our wages, except the men who employ us, and they only by mutual agreement and consent. We did not delegate that right to you. A great majority of our employers have no connection or affiliation, and we may add, no sympathy with the men who did appoint you.
>
> We are informed by many legitimate contractors that they have been forced out of business. . . .
>
> Hundreds of our employers, reputable business men, have been forced during the last fifteen months to go hat in hand to a combination of material dealers for a permit to secure material in order that they might carry on their legitimate business. They have been forced to remove sub-contractors from the jobs because they employed union men. They have been forced to discharge their old and trusted union employees in order to secure material. . . .
>
> We stand squarely on the proposition, sir, that the building contractor has the sole right to determine who he shall employ, and the right to go into conference with us and negotiate an agreement specifying the minimum wage he shall pay. . . .
>
> In conclusion, we . . . decline to become parties to the autocratic attempt of your board to determine wages . . . .

San Francisco's carpenters went on strike against the American Plan in April, 1926. The Industrial Association trotted out "Black Jack" Jerome and his assorted goons, who promptly slugged a disabled veteran because he would not break a strike. When three carpenters were arrested for allegedly assaulting a non-union man named Louis McDermott, the latter admitted under cross-examination that he was an ex-con from the East who came to San

Francisco to break the strike. Another heavy admitted that he was offered $50 for each union man that he beat up.

The strike dragged on. President Hutcheson visited San Francisco, making several vain attempts to settle it. Several contractors were willing, but the Association resisted anything that smacked of collective bargaining, even turning thumbs down on mediation.

Hutcheson then developed an unusual line of attack, designed to take advantage of an employer arrangement. San Francisco contractors were required to obtain permits from the Builders Exchange in order to purchase materials. The condition for obtaining a permit was adherence to the American Plan. It was, in truth, a beautiful scheme though clearly a restraint of trade. The U.S. Supreme Court, however, declared it constitutional, ruling in effect that there was no interstate commerce involved to restrain. When it was pointed out that no plaster was produced within the state, the court found that the plaster was "comingled with the common mass of local property" after its interstate journey.

If that is the name of the game, Hutcheson reasoned, that is the game we will play. The Brotherhood went into the building supply business. It imported cement from Belgium, purchased lumber from independent mills, bought and operated rock quarries and gravel beds. Contractors willing to employ union workers were able to circumvent the American Plan hold over building supplies. By February, 1927, the Brotherhood was in a position to talk turkey with eager builders and contractors. The Brotherhood got out of the building supply business, and the American Plan began to disintegrate.

And not only in San Francisco. In 1928, the National Association of Manufacturers complained that the open shop gains of the 1920s were all but wiped out by union efforts. Standing before the delegates to the Brotherhood's 1928 convention, Hutcheson reported, "while there are still periodical attempts . . . to put into effect the open shop . . . [we] have been able to combat these efforts so that the system has not become anything other than what might be termed 'Local:' only existing in a few localities."

It was no mean achievement.

VIII

THE DISMAL DECADE

The early warning signals began flashing in *The Carpenter* as early as mid-1928.—"work is very scarce in Kansas City . . . conditions in Lawrence, Mass. are very bad . . . Akron advises that work in that vicinity is very scarce . . . very little work in Plainfield, New Jersey . . . Many men walking the streets . . . in San Francisco . . . All carpenters are requested to steer clear. . . ."

"We, as a nation," *The Carpenter* warned in August, 1929, "are facing a situation that is phenomenal, in that while we have abundant resources, a vast accumulation of capital and equipment, and large numbers of highly energetic, highly-skilled workers capable of more production than at any time in the history of civilization, yet, millions of workers do not have an opportunity for regular and steady work."

Two months later, on October 29, the stock market boom collapsed, bringing the rest of the economy down with a sharp tumble. Unemployment began to mount at the rate of 4,000 a week. National income, which had topped 87 billion dollars in 1929, fell to 41.7 billion dollars in 1932. The Federal Reserve Board index of manufacturing production slid from 110 in 1929 to 57 in 1932. Total new construction, which peaked at $20.8-million in 1929, bottomed at $6.6-million in 1933. Wage payments shrivelled from 50 billion dollars to 30 billion dollars. Unemployment rose—four million in 1930, 11 million in 1932, nearly 13 million in 1933. Brotherhood Secretary Frank Duffy reported that less than thirty percent of the members were employed.

Carpenters, like most Americans, were bewildered by the rapid turn of economic events. Nonetheless, they were eager, as the pages of *The Carpenter* amply demonstrate, to analyze the crisis, and discuss possible solutions.

"Facts are facts," Peter A. Reilly of Boston wrote, "and to discuss them openly in our official journal is, in my mind, better than discussing them on the curbstone and in secret conspiring places."

Editor Frank Duffy apparently agreed, for he gave correspondents free reign, excepting, of course, Moscow-directed Communists. Reilly, for example, touched upon an issue particularly sensitive to trade union leadership. "A gulf between the union worker and the union officer," he wrote, "seems to exist and is widening and deepening as the years go by." He was disappointed that an article by A. F. of L. President Green on unemployment and machine displacement had not offered a definite remedy. "He is in a position to devote considerable time to a deliberation and solution to this question, and, naturally, we who help pay him expect constructive, wholesome and practical advice from him."

Green and Reilly, however, were one in agreeing that the cause of unemployment was in the increased use of machinery, in changing technology. "The house carpenter," Lyman Wisely of Coulterville, Illinois wrote, "who less than two decades ago needed several hundred dollars worth of tools, is even now in competition with any handy man, who, according to the ads, needs only the blueprints we furnish free, a hammer, screw driver and a little spare-time to erect his own home." But it was not only the do-it-yourself advertisements that flourished in *Popular Mechanics* and like publications that worried skilled mechanics. Every carpenter was familiar with the developments listed by another *Carpenter* correspondent: "Mortising machines for locking doors; where one man can do in one day, more work than five used to do. The power hand saw, used for all kinds of rough cutting on the job; where one man can do more cutting of wood in one day than ten men ordinarily would do. The use of electric hand machines that will enable one man to drill and bore more holes in wood in one day, then ten men used to do. The power floor surfacing machine that surfaces more floor in a day with one or two men than a dozen would ordinarily do with the old hand scraping method."

The writer conceded all the advantages of machinery but, then asked, "are we not confronted with the perplexing problem of employment for the vast number of mechanics who are consequently thrown out of work?"

Responses ranged from those who bemoaned specialization in the trade and those who welcomed it, those who favored restricting memberships and those who did not. Charles S. Stone, Sr., of Webster Grove, Missouri, condemned "the system of the bosses which has permitted them to so divide the trade that the men never get a chance to learn but one thing." And Walter B. Stevenson, an old-timer from Cortland, New York, grumbled, "there are carpenters . . . [who] could not tell a hypothenuse from the square root of a hog's nose." He urged that the Borterhood refrain from taking in apprentices for a reasonable period of time and raise the initiation fee for new members. Several urged that permits for traveling members be tightened up, even denied so long as resident carpenters were unemployed. Others urged a universal examination to establish proficiency and licensing by the state as electricians and plumbers were licensed.

The debate over specialization, the uses of machinery, drew the greatest sparks. "Brother Wisely," William Jamieson of Ontario, Canada, declared, "defines progress thus—a carpenter becomes a form-builder, a joist-setter, bridging-butter and nailer, a floor-layer, partition-setter, door-fitter, door-hanger, hardware putters-on, roofers, etc. This writer would call that 'Regression' and any trade unionist who would allow himself to be pushed back to such a degree has little respect for himself as a man and is unworthy of the name of a skilled mechanic." Brother Wisely was urged to hold on to his steel square for "it has been in use now for thousands of years, the Samaritans used it long before the flood, Noah handled it for forty years while building the Ark. The workers on the Tower of Babel laid their work out with it, the Babylonians carried it in their tool box. The Egyptians had to use it to the run and rise of Sphinx's nose, it was in constant use on Solomon's Temple, The Carpenter of Nazareth was familiar with it . . . When Brother Wisely's dust and the writer's is being blown about by the stormy winds that blow, the steel square will still be called for and used."

Brother Wisely, naturally, rose to the bait, remarking that the steel square accounts for the Tower of Babel. "Looking back, one can see that bunch start on the job jabbering about how to file saws and, as the building nears the wall plates, they get out their new patent squares, with the rafter tables on 'em and start babbling about roof framing. It's no wonder the job went blooey." As for Solomon's Temple, "that was the first 'readicut' job in Jerusalem. . . . It took 3,300 bosses and about 170,000 'stone squarers,' wood hewers and burden bearers about seven years to readicut that job, whereas with pneumatic stone dressers, gang-saws and truck service, about 17 men would complete a job of that size before the ladies auxiliary could make arrangements to serve the banquet at the grand opening."

Behind the debate, the often sharp exchanges, one senses a need for, and a reliance on the Brotherhood in a trying time. Most carpenters, after all, recognized, as G. W. Ahner of Yuba City, California, put it, "This is an age of specialization; if you do not specialize in some branch of carpentry, you are simply out of luck." And agreed with Ira D. Kneeland of Prather, California, who observed, "these machines are here to stay . . . the task [is to make] them function for the welfare of all mankind, not for the financial aggrandizement of a few." At a time when there were no unemployment or social security benefits, when economic depression aggravated job displacement by technological change, they wanted protection by their union.

Peter A. Reilly accurately assessed the situation when he wrote, in the winter of 1930, "Whether or not that protection shall come through a restrictive membership policy, or through an increased business policy, is debatable. It has been considered pro and con by the various officers of the Brotherhood without any large degree of unanimity among them. Various districts have attempted the membership limitation as a corrective for the labor surplus problem in our trade. Its validity has been questioned by prospective candidates, and appeals taken to the General Office, and the candidate sustained in his protest."

What the Brotherhood could do, it did well. Even with a considerable drop in membership—down to a low of 242,000 in 1932 and with upwards of one third unable to pay dues—the Brotherhood was able to pay over 1928–1940 close to $12-million in benefits—including $7-million for death and disability, and nearly $5-million in pensions.

At the onset of the Depression, Brotherhood President Hutcheson along with A. F. of L. President Green and key labor leaders such as John Frey and Frank Morrison, met with President Hoover, who secured their support for a Federal Public Building Program. He, in turn, obtained Hutcheson's backing to aid and stimulate the building and construction industries in so far as it was within the Brotherhood's power to do so.

The Brotherhood also carried on a desperate struggle to hold the line on union scales. It helped to secure the passage of the Davis-Bacon Act in 1930, which forestalled wage-cutting in the public sector through application of the prevailing wage on federally-aided construction. "On every hand, wage cuts were demanded by employers," Hutcheson told the delegates to the Brotherhood's 1936 convention. "Our members resisted these efforts to tear down their established conditions to the limit of their ability. Many changes were forced upon us, but few were conceded. Our members refused to believe that low wages would create work. . . . While sheer poverty made it impossible for many thousands of our members to pay dues, they never lost or surrendered their union principles."

As the Brotherhood celebrated its Golden Jubilee, it pressed the struggle for shorter hours and a shorter work week as an answer to unemployment. Chicago carpenters, as an example, established the five-day week in December, 1930. "It does appear," stated the authoritative Carpenters Monthly Bulletin early in 1931, "in so far as the United States and Canada are concerned, the carpenters are out in front securing the five-day week, and it is very regrettable that in some of the smaller towns the full day six-day week is still

Depression

the accepted custom." Seven years later, the Fair Labor Standards
Act established a maximum 40-hour week. But the Brotherhood
had led the way.

In March, 1932, Carpenter Locals in Chicago, through the
District Council, petitioned the Brotherhood General Office to
secure the cooperation of the A. F. of L. in urging Congress to vote
for immediate financial relief for the unemployed and to enact a
plan for Unemployment Insurance. It was the beginning of a drive
that culminated in the Social Security Act of 1935, which established
our present system of unemployment compensation and old-age
pensions.

The Brotherhood, however, was chary of government, which,
after all, had a record of intervention on the side of employers in

labor matters. Hutcheson, who was a major figure in the A. F. of L. executive council was in considerable measure responsible for the Federation's reluctance to endorse wholeheartedly New Deal measures. As late as 1937, Hutcheson opposed, unsuccessfully in this instance, A. F. of L. endorsement of pending minimum wage legislation. In the depths of the recession, as Philip Taft has pointed out, the Federation continued to think in terms of employment and income rather than in terms of relief and aid. As the depression dragged on, the Federation changed its position on unemployment insurance and other such measures.*

The Depression was too deep for individuals, even for great and powerful unions, to overcome. Financially-pinched, carpenters voted in referendum 33,280 to 22,598 to postpone the 1932 convention.

Men over 40 were deemed too old to work at their trade. The Brotherhood, on April 19, 1932, took the unprecedented step of allowing local unions to carry members twelve months before reporting them suspended. Many Locals provided benefits for unemployed members equal to dues, so that they could remain in good standing and not lose out on union benefits.

"Ours may be the first nation to go to the poorhouse in an automobile," cracked humorist Will Rogers. But, he added, correctly assessing the nation's mood, "you let this country go hungry and they are going to eat, no matter what happens to budgets, Income Taxes or Wall Street values. Washington mustn't forget who rules when it comes to a showdown."

In retrospect, it appears that the whole country must have supported Franklin D. Roosevelt against Herbert Hoover in 1932. But that was not the case. Hutcheson served as chairman of the

---

* Frank Duffy cited the Federation's objections to certain compulsory features common to such plans in Great Britain and Germany then being upheld as a model for the United States. Workers in Great Britain, for example, were compelled to take "suitable employment" or lose their benefits. "We find," Frank Wolstencroft, General Secretary of the Amalgamated workers of Great Britain, informed the 1931 A. F. of L. convention, "that in the majority of the cases in which the Court of Appeals decides the appeals as to whether a person is entitled to benefits or not, there are two to one against the workman . . ."

Depositors trying to retrieve their money during the bank crash of the depression.

Labor Bureau of the Republican National Committee, and through his efforts the Republican party pledged itself "to continue its efforts to maintain this present standards of living and high wage scale."

Hutcheson and the Building Trades Department of the A. F. of L. endorsed Hoover; the Federation declared itself non-partisan. When Local Union 58 of Chicago protested Hucheson's role in the Republican Party, the General Executive Board noted that he had accepted the position as an individual. "This is the privilege of any member of the organization," the G.E.B. declared, holding to the Brotherhood's tradition of no politics within the union. One surmises that many carpenters, perhaps most, voted for Franklin D. Roosevelt.

There is no question but that the country was in the mood for a change; certainly it was looking for a way out of the Depression. The National Industrial Recovery Act (NIRA), signed by President

Roosevelt on June 16, 1933, was designed "to put people back to work." Industry and labor were encouraged by government to cooperate in order to stimulate recovery. Codes were drawn up. The model code barred child labor under 16 years of age, established a 40-hour work week for white collar workers and 35 hours for factory workers or artisans, and a 40-cent-an-hour minimum wage. Most important for organized labor, Section 7a guaranteed the right to bargain and Section 7b imposed on the President the responsibility of encouraging mutual agreements between employees and employers on the maximum hours of labor, minimum rates of pay, and other conditions of employment. Such agreements were to be a part of the NRA (National Recovery Administration) codes.

"The National Industrial Recovery Act," *The Carpenter* declared in August, 1933, "gives a golden opportunity to employees in the Northwest to organize themselves into bona fide trade unions." It was a sentiment widely shared among trade unionists. Yet, other interpretations were possible. Employers in the Northwest lumber industry—and elsewhere, too—were attempting to exclude unions from the framing of codes, in this instance, by giving sole recognition to an outfit called the Loyal Legion of Loggers, a company union. It soon became apparent that the NIRA was not all that unions had hoped for from the new Administration in Washington. Hutcheson charged, as an instance, that NRA authorities approved attempts to lower wage scales already agreed to in direct negotiations between the Brotherhood and the employers.

Criticism of the NRA, however, was made moot by the Supreme Court, which held the NIRA unconstitutional in 1935. Unhappily, labor's right-to-bargain toe-hold—Section 7a—also went by the board. Labor, however, responded to the challenge. The Brotherhood and other A. F. of L. unions joined forces to win support in Congress for what became popularly known as the Wagner Labor Act, after its Senate sponsor Robert F. Wagner, Democrat Senator from New York. Enacted in July, 1935 and held constitutional by the Supreme Court two years later in March, 1937, the National Labor Relations Act guaranteed workers the right to organize, to bargain collectively through representatives of their own choosing. Actions by employers interfering with organization or refusing to bargain were defined as unfair labor practices. Truly, organized labor now had a Magna Carta.

Nonetheless, this did not mean that labor's struggles were now over. In a sense, they had just begun, only the ground rules were now enforced by government and were a good deal fairer. The question of so-called "independent" unions had yet to be resolved. Still, in truth, the future of the labor movement was to be decided by organization and that rested on the outcome of a growing division within the House of Labor.

Though the Brotherhood lost members during the depths of the Depression, it also added new members. In 1930, for example, the Associated Millwrights of America, a union of flour and cereal mill spouters with headquarters in Buffalo, New York, joined the Brotherhood. Chicago millmen met in February, 1934, to boost the Brotherhood among mill workers within a five hundred mile radius of Chicago. It was just one of many steps taken to strengthen the Brotherhood among millmen nationally. Furniture workers were organized on the West Coast and elsewhere during the mid-1930s. Plywood and veneer workers joined; union-made plywood now carried the union label for the first time. But the Brotherhood's major organization effort in the 1930s, without a doubt, was among the lumber and sawmill workers, particularly in the Pacific Northwest.

Ox teams and skid roads were being replaced by steel-spar skidders, sky-line cables, power saws, steam, electric and diesel engines in penetrating ever deeper into the primeval forests of the Northwest. High-climbers wired twelve sticks of dynamite in a ring around giant trunks (sliding down fifty feet to await the explosion) to topple a three-ton tree top. On the foaming Clearwater River in Idaho, 100 sure-footed Paul Bunyans drove enough logs to the mill each spring to build a city. From Clatskanie, Oregon, two or more giant log rafts—each with 5,000,000 feet of timber—were floated 1,100 miles each summer down the Pacific Coast to San Diego.

The woodsmen were a rough, tough breed. Living conditions in the camps were often deplorable; wages were as low as ten cents an hour before World War I. Organizing was difficult because the men moved often and the camps were a long way from town. The Wobblies, members of the Industrial Workers of the World, organized "free-speech" drives as a way of catching loggers' attention when they did come to town. Their efforts to organize were bitterly resisted by the employers, and there were a number of pitched battles, with casualties on both sides, in the years bracketing the First World War. The Wobblies' anarcho-syndicalist philosophy was unpalatable to most wood workers and aroused a good deal of public hostility, which contributed to the collapse of the IWW in

the 1920s. The American Federation of Labor managed to organize a handful of federal locals of lumber, timber and sawmill workers in the Northwest, some 7,500 workers in all. At its February, 1935 meeting, the A. F. of L. Executive Council decided to turn these Federal locals and the jurisdiction over to the Brotherhood.

"We got busy," Frank Duffy later recalled. "We sent one of our board members to the Northwest and some ten or twelve organizers; we sent organizers to the middle states, to the southern states, with the result that at the end of fourteen months we had 130,000 of these men in our organization. We entered into agreements with the big lumber barons of the Northwest. We got increased wages for them, we got shorter hours, we got better working conditions for them. . . . We thought that in fourteen months we had made a big gain."

The gain was scored at the cost of a major strike. In May, 1935, ten thousand workers left logging camps and sawmills of Western Oregon and Western Washington, demanding union recognition. By the middle of the month, over 30,000 were out. Negotiations with two of the biggest mill operators achieved a breakthrough, the forty-hour week and a 50-cents-an-hour minimum wage with proportionate increases for greater skills. But settlements were delayed and the walkout lengthened by a month through the machinations of the Communists active in the Pacific Northwest. It was an ill omen.

The Brotherhood, of course, was not deterred by Communist efforts at disruption, nor did it rest on its laurels. "We had yet 250,000 men to organize," Frank Duffy observed. "We had men on the job. We didn't expect interference from any organization, but we were interfered with."

What happened? The Brotherhood had run afoul of the ambitions of John L. Lewis, Communist scheming, and the rise of the Congress of Industrial Organizations (CIO).

As the country picked its way out of the slough of the Depression, workers took heart and began to organize. New opportunities developed for unionization in the auto, rubber, steel and other so-called mass production industries. This caused debate among trade unionists.

"Experience has shown," the 1934 A. F. of L. convention declared, "that craft organization is most effective in protecting the welfare and advancing the interests of workers where the nature of the industry is such that lines of demarcation between crafts are distinguishable." But, added the convention, "in many of the industries in which thousands of workers are employed a new condition exists requiring organization upon a different basis to be most effective."

The Federation, in a sense, confronted a situation analogous to that the Brotherhood faced some twenty years before when it had to organize millmen. The organization of inside carpenters called for a somewhat different approach than used in organizing outside carpenters. The same was true of organizing the lumber and sawmill workers. The Brotherhood had two classifications of membership: those who paid full dues and received full benefits, and non-beneficial members (130,000 at the time), who received no benefits. Non-beneficial locals set their own dues and paid a monthly tax of only 25 cents per member to the General Officers; beneficial members paid 75 cents. (Carpenters, in 1939, averaged 75 cents to $1 an hour; lumber workers, 50 cents.) However, the Constitution then provided: "To be elected as a general officer a member must be a full beneficial member." Therefore, only beneficial members were eligible as convention delegates. This, naturally, was an irritant and, some suspected, a block to organization. The General Executive Board recognized the problem in the mid-1930s and concluded that it would be helpful to have non-beneficial Locals represented at the Convention by fraternal delegates. But the Board was unwilling to set aside or even to propose amending the constitution. "All they have to do," Duffy informed 1936 convention delegates, "is ask for a beneficial charter, comply with our laws, pay the initiation fee, pay the dues . . . pay the tax to headquarters, and nobody can question their right to sit in the convention."

This may seem harsh, but the non-beneficial members did benefit from Brotherhood support. Thousands of dollars, for example, were spent in organizing the lumber and sawmill workers in the Northwest. The Brotherhood also picked up a major share of court costs in a crucial Seattle case. When timber workers went on strike in Omak, Washington, sixteen months of picketing exhausted a life-time of savings. School children were ragged and barefoot. The Brotherhood appropriated strike aid.

To meet the new conditions confronting workers in the mass production industries, the 1934 A. F. of L. convention instructed the Executive Council to use its judgment as to form of organization and jurisdictional limitations. With this in mind, charters were issued for national unions in the auto and rubber industries.

The Brotherhood did not oppose new organizational efforts, but it did feel the need to protect craftsmen from exploitation. Auto manufacturers, for example, not only used their employees to maintain building equipment but also on new construction, and at far less wages than building trades' pay scales. "If it is an admitted fact that the A. F. of L. has been brought to the point it has," Hutcheson told his confreres on the Executive Council, "through following the lines of craftsmanship, I think we should adhere to that with the thought in mind of protecting these craftsmen and at the same time give these men [in auto] an opportunity to organize; but I do not believe we should give them a charter so broad that they can go out and claim any employee that might be employed by these automobile manufacturers."*

But the advocates of industrial unionism were not satisfied. John L. Lewis rose at the 1935 A. F. of L. convention in Atlantic City to decry the Federation's organizational efforts. "This convention," he declared, "is teeming with delegates from these industries

---

* What the Brotherhood had in mind as a way of resolving the difficulty referred to by Hutcheson may have been its agreement on jurisdiction with the United Mine Workers, made in 1914:

"That all carpenters working as handy men employed permanently, or handy men employed in and about the mines, whether repairing or constructing in any capacity, shall be members of the United Mine Workers of America.

"That all carpenters employed in building or rebuilding breakers, tipples, washers, houses, or other buildings, shall be members of the United Brotherhood of Carpenters and Joiners of America."

where those unions [federal labor unions] have been established and where they are now dying like grass withering before the autumn sun, who are ready to tell this convention of the need for that change in policy. . . . Today, the craft unions may be able to stand upon their own feet and, like mighty oaks before the gale, defy the lightning. The day may come when this changed scheme of things—and things are rapidly changing now—the day may come when these organizations will not be able to withstand the lightning and the gale. Prepare yourselves by making a contribution to your less fortunate brethren. Heed this cry from Macedonia that comes from the hearts of men: Organize the unorganized."

Lewis's dramatic plea, however, failed to move the convention to adopt his industrial union policy. Later, when the question came up in the guise of a resolution authorizing a charter for the Rubber Workers, Hutcheson rose to a point of order, "the industrial union question has been previously settled by this convention." After exchanges between the chair and other delegates, Lewis raised his own point of order, remarking at the end, "This thing of raising points of order all the time on minor delegates is rather small potatoes."

Smarting, Hutcheson rose again. "I was raised on small potatoes. That is why I am so small."

Lewis walked up the aisle, a hush fell over the convention. He paused before Hutcheson, whose six feet three inches overshadowed even Lewis's formidable 225-pound frame.

Lewis muttered a profanity. Hutcheson replied in kind. Lewis stiffened; suddenly cracked Hutcheson on the cheek. The two grappled, going down amidst the clatter of collapsing chairs as delegates struggled to separate them.*

---

* Lewis and Hutcheson, who had been friends, resumed their friendship a few years later. Both were Republicans. Lewis supported a Democrat only in 1936. Both endorsed Wendell Wilkie, the Republican candidate in 1940, and opposed a third term for Roosevelt. Hutcheson also backed Lewis's efforts to end A. F. of L. and CIO rivalry during World War II and he was the chief backer of Lewis when the United Mine Workers re-affiliated with the Federation in 1946. When Lewis feared that the Mine Workers would lose their treasury as a consequence of fines imposed during a 1945 walkout, he asked Hutcheson to hold

It was, surely, the most celebrated exchange of blows in the history of labor. It certainly dramatized the subsequent break-a-way of the CIO unions from the House of Labor. Which, of course, appeared to be John L.'s purpose.

Dual unionism is a trade union sin. The Brotherhood did not object to the organizing of the unorganized, even across muddied jurisdictional lines, but it did object to CIO raiding. In the Northwest, the CIO chartered the International Woodworkers of America. "Why didn't they organize the 250,000 that were yet to be organized?" Frank Duffy asked. "If they had done that I would not have said a word, but to take away the men we had organized I will fight to the bitter end."

Though relations between the two organizations are now amicable, they did fight it out—almost to the bitter end—down through the 1940s.

The fraternal delegates from the Northwestern sawmill and lumber workers locals at the 1936 Brotherhood convention were discontented; they wanted full-voting rights and two seats on the Brotherhood's General Executive Board. After a Board subcommittee meeting with the Northwest delegates, it was agreed, and the convention approved the course of action, that a subcommittee of the Board would make a first-hand survey of the industry, that a union label would be designed for use on all logs; that nine firms then on strike would be placed on the Brotherhood's "We Don't Patronize List," and that an organizing campaign would be continued with organizers who spoke the language of and understood the industry.

However, the lumber and sawmill delegates were not satisfied; they stopped off on the way home to meet with John L. Lewis. Initially, nothing much came of this meeting since Lewis appeared not to be interested in organizing woodworkers in the Northwest.

---

in safekeeping—and without bond—the U.M.W. certified check, made out to Hutcheson, for $1,000,000. "Bill Hutcheson was in the million dollar class as far as the United Mine Workers and I were concerned," Lewis told an interviewer many years later.

Meanwhile, the Communist Party had changed its line, from penetration of mainstream labor organizations such as the Brotherhood to support of the break-a-way CIO. Communists working among the lumber and sawmill workers were now instructed to pull out of the Brotherhood as many lumber and sawmill local unions as they could manage. By then, in mid-1937, the CIO was openly raiding the Brotherhood in the Northwest. Harold Pritchett, a Canadian who turned out to be a blind follower of the Communists, showed up to lead the secession with $50,000 at his disposal from the CIO.

When the Northwest woodsmen met, in June, 1937, the CIO sent John Brophy and Harry Bridges to urge secession. Brotherhood organizer Abe Muir denounced CIO dual unionism; but he could not hold the line solid. By mid-July, approximately 35 percent of the membership had seceded from the Brotherhood to join the IWA.

"The CIO has challenged us," Hutcheson wrote in a special bulletin issued in the fall of 1937, "and we must meet that challenge without hesitation." Brotherhood local unions and councils were instructed to appoint a committee to inform employers and the lumber dealers that members would refuse to handle any dual or CIO products.

The struggle between the Brotherhood and the I.W.A. raged like a forest fire on the timbered slopes of Northwestern mountains. A disgusted public enacted, in Oregon, an anti-labor law by referendum. Though later struck down along with similar statutes by the U.S. Supreme Court, the damage was done. By 1940, the dispute had simmered down, though it continued until the I.W.A. shed its Communists and a measure of stability returned to the industry in the post-World War II period.

At the 1940 convention, Hutcheson reported that 35,000 lumber and sawmill workers were working under closed-shop agreements. Several thousand others belonged to the Brotherhood, but were not under closed-shop agreements. "We were hampered in our efforts," Hutcheson added, "due to the fact that, shortly after our last convention, a group that was affiliated with the Locals and chartered by the Brotherhood left the organization, and affiliated with the CIO. They called themselves the International Wood-workers of America, and while, for a time, they caused our members a great deal of annoyance and inconvenience, I am gratified to inform you that the representatives of our members report that we are making very material and substantial progress, and that the group which seceded from our organization is gradually diminishing."*

Actually, the Brotherhood had survived a dismal decade. At its close, Frank Duffy observed, "We organized 409 unions since the last convention. . . . We added 20,000 to our membership. Times were not so good during the past four years, and I think that is a good record. Times are different now. I suppose the number of our local unions (2,315 in the States and Canada) now will reach 2,500 and that our membership (then 313,848) . . . will reach nearly 400,000."

---

* At the time, the I.W.A. claimed a membership of 100,000, but its true membership was closer to 25,000. The internecine warfare, in truth, had not helped to organize the woodsmen of the Northwest.

IX

THE FIGHTING CARPENTERS

Carpenters, Frank Duffy told delegates at the Brotherhood's 1940 convention, have been known from colonial days down to the present time as the "Fighting Carpenters."

Duffy's spirited combativeness was justified. The Brotherhood was in the courts battling anti-trust injunctions—and winning. It was organizing. It was growing. But there was a graver side; for, as Duffy also remarked, "Carpenters are in the first-line trenches right now, in the building of cantonments in the camps, in the forts, in the aviation fields, in the ship-building yards—wherever the government wants them they are there by the thousands and they will stay there as long as the government needs them."

Canadian members were already at war. Hitler and Stalin had divided Poland, the Germans were at the Channel, and the RAF contested the Luftwaffe for control of the skies. The United States prepared for the worst. It was a hectic period of preparedness, struggling against time, praying that American initiative and industrial genius would overcome in a few scant months Hitler's seven years' preparation of the vast military machine that was terrorizing Europe.

Trade unionists, particularly Carpenters, were early opponents of totalitarianism, black or red. *The Carpenter* exposed the evil of Bolshevism from the first and denounced the rise of Hitler. When the German democratic trade union movement was crushed by the Nazis in early 1933, the Carpenters joined an A. F. of L. call for a boycott "until the German government recognizes the right of the working people of Germany to organize into bona fide, independent trade unions of their own choosing, and until Germany ceases its repressive policy of persecution of the Jewish people."

As a guest speaker at the 1940 Brotherhood convention, George Meany, then Secretary-Treasurer of the A. F. of L., drew a lesson that he would stress throughout his life. "The history of totalitarianism," he said, "and the record of dictatorships show that when the trade union movement is destroyed civil liberties are wiped out. There are some who believe that this war of preparedness, this emergency, should be used to take from the trade unions some of the prerogatives that they have had in the past. Let them take warning from this fact, that if the right to assemble, the right to gather together in order to improve conditions one for the other—and after all, that is all that a trade union is—if that right is destroyed, then let me say . . . that all other rights . . . will similarly be destroyed—the right to go to church and worship God according to the dictates of your own conscience, the right to meet in civic organizations, the right to assemblege—all those rights naturally run parallel to the right of working men to meet and exercise the principles and policies of trade unionism."

Trade unions, Meany added, "have a responsibility to protect the standards of life, and to protect above all the freedom guaranteed under our Constitution . . . depend on our trade union organizations to carry us through this crisis—and when I say 'us' I mean this great nation of ours, because unless the trade union movement . . . stands up and co-operates to the fullest extent, democracy cannot be preserved in this country."

Meany had cause for his concern, for the labor movement was under attack. Representative Howard W. Smith of Virginia introduced a bill shortly before the convention that, in Hutcheson's graphic phrase, would "hog-tie" workers defending themselves. Hutcheson drafted a carefully phrased resolution that endorsed United States defense efforts, expressed "Sympathy with the principles of those provisions in Mr. Smith's bill which propose to punish severely such acts of sabotage, violence and betrayal," and condemned "those provisions . . . which seek to strike down and revoke the traditional rights of labor" as "unnecessary, oppressive and destructive of the very liberty which the program of national defense is designed to protect." The delegates, at Hutcheson's suggestion, took an unprecedented step, not satisfied with just adopting the resolution, each one signed it. "I thought," Hutcheson said, "perhaps it would be more effective with the representatives in Congress if it were signed by the delegates from the various districts." The resolution was signed by individual delegates before it was introduced for adoption, and the Committee on Resolution added a recommendation that the delegates, once back home, get their members to urge their Congressmen to vote against the measure.

The attack on labor, however, was not confined to Congress. Thurman Arnold, then assistant attorney-general of the United States in charge of the anti-trust division, declared war on what he termed "bottle necks of business." Among the so-called bottle necks, in Arnold's view, were "unreasonable restraints" imposed by "unjustified" strikes. Invoking the Sherman Anti-Trust Act, Arnold and his men went before eleven grand juries and secured indictments against the leaders of 81 unions, including the Brotherhood, the Teamsters, the Longshoremen, Stonecutters, Painters, Distillery Workers and the Typographers. He then cajoled and intimidated the unions, particularly the weaker ones, into "consent decrees." The brunt of battle fell to the Carpenters.

"Mr. Arnold," Hutcheson declared, "is endeavoring to bring about a condition so that he might act as a referee or arbiter in any dispute which may arise. What the representatives of this administration are trying to do is to place labor organizations directly under their direction, so that they might tell us what we can do and when we can do it." The Carpenters would have none of it.

Seven indictments were handed down in 1940 against the Brotherhood and its officers. In Pittsburgh, the charges alleged interference by members of the union with the shipment in Allegheny County of stock millwork made outside the county. It also alleged that the Brotherhood denied permission to millwork manufacturers to use the union label because they had agreements with the CIO Woodworkers. The Chicago indictment charged that

the Brotherhood called strikes to assist in the carrying out of
". . . [a] conspiracy to interfere with a shipment of cut stone from
outside of Chicago into the city of Chicago." On the west coast,
the Brotherhood was accused of a conspiracy to prevent Harbor
Plywood Corporation from selling douglas fir plywood in the state
of Washington for shipment into other states. The Bay Counties
District Council was indicted for having "control of the supply of
workmen available for the installation of millwork and patterned
lumber in the San Francisco Bay area. . . ." But the whole anti-
trust case was to rise and fall on the 1939 criminal indictment of
Hutcheson and three St. Louis Carpenters' officers—George Casper
Ottens, John A. Callahan and Joseph August Klein—for a criminal
conspiracy to restrain interstate commerce.

Arnold went to court to urge that any jurisdictional dispute
was, in and of itself, a violation of the Sherman Anti-Trust Act. As
Brotherhood attorney in the case, Charles H. Tuttle, a prominent
Wall Street lawyer, remarked, "Call a thing a jurisdictional dispute
and you have got a crime. . . ."

The St. Louis indictment was, indeed, based on a long-
standing jurisdictional dispute between the Carpenters and the
Machinists. Both unions had an agreement with Anheuser-Busch,
the well-known brewery, but the craft lines were neither clearly
drawn nor mutually agreed upon. So, when Anheuser-Busch
decided to erect a new tank building in its St. Louis plant and gave
the work on the machinery entirely to the machinists, the Brotherhood protested and then called a strike of the millwrights and
carpenters inside the plant. As Tuttle later described it, "It was a
common, ordinary, garden variety kind of strike. The millwrights
and carpenters walked out. They put up umbrellas. I don't think
it was raining, but they put up umbrellas that said that the Anheuser-
Busch company was unfair to labor. . . . And what seemed to hurt
Mr. Arnold almost more than anything else, they included [in a
declaration published in *The Carpenter*] a suggestion that the friends
of labor should refrain from drinking Anheuser-Busch for awhile."

The boycott apparently irritated Mr. Arnold more than it did
the country's beer drinkers, for he charged that it was a conspiracy
to drive the beer company from the interstate market. If he could

make the charge stick, it would nullify the Clayton and the Norris-LaGuardia Acts which specifically exempted unions from anti-trust actions. This would mean a return to the era of the injunction, a severe crippling of labor's right to strike. If unions came within the purview of the Sherman Anti-Trust Act, then government could regulate union practices as well as those of the employers.

Since Arnold launched his attack in 1939, thirty-eight indicted unions had spent $2,000,000 in defense. Six paid $130,000 in fines and nine had taken Arnold's advice, pleading *nolo contendere*. "Big Bill" was invited to a series of luncheons with the trust-buster, but neither cajolery nor threats budged Hutcheson. Brotherhoood attorneys appeared in the St. Louis District Court—and won! The government's case was dismissed.

Furious, Arnold appealed the case in the United States Supreme Court. It was argued before the high court on December 10, 1940. On February 3, 1941, with Justice Felix Frankfurter delivering the majority opinion, the court dismissed the indictment. In sum, it upheld the injunction exemptions of the Clayton and Norris LaGuardia acts. The carpenters refusal to stop work was not a crime, nor was it criminal to ask people not to drink Anheuser-Busch beer. Congress did not exclude jurisdictional disputes from the immunities granted to organized labor by the Clayton Act. The unions finally secured effective relief from many attacks under the Sherman Act.

It was a landmark labor decision. As Hutcheson spelled it out later: "It was and has been the first case and forerunner of all decisions affecting labor, on the right to picket, the right to boycott, the right to circulate statements, the right to assume and maintain jurisdiction, the right to persuade other trades to quit with us, the right to call strikes on other jobs and the right to enforce our laws as made by the membership of the Brotherhood."

When the Japanese attacked Pearl Harbor, the startled station commander quickly recovered and sent out a call over the Honolulu radio for all yard workers to report at once. By the time the second wave of bombers rained their deadly cargo on the hapless base, the streets in the Navy Yard were thick with incoming carpenters, other building tradesmen and metal trades workers. "Instead of running to cover," a Naval officer later reported, "they ran to their jobs. Lots of them were shaking their fists in the air."

In that spirit, the Brotherhood responded to the outbreak of war. Gordon C. Bond, a member of Van Nuys Local 1913, a civilian worker employed on Wake Island died "in action," fighting the invaders. He was among the first carpenter casualties during World War II. Some seventy-five thousand Brotherhood members served in the armed forces, many in the famed Seabees, the construction regiments of the Navy engaged to build advance and mobile bases overseas. There were heroes: Technical Sergeant Meyer Cohen of Philadelphia Local 277, awarded the Distinguished Flying Cross as a gunner-engineer in the 15th AAF. He helped to bring back a badly shot-up bomber. Captain Frank A. Cutler, a member of Cleveland Local 11, became an Ace, credited with ten Nazi planes before being reported missing in action somewhere over Europe. Torger Tokle, champion skier and a member of New York/New Jersey Dock Builders Local 1456, joined the Tenth Mountain Division. As a platoon sergeant, he led his men up a mountainside the Germans considered unscalable. Killed by a shell fragment, late winter, 1945, he was among the last carpenter casualties of the war.

On the home front, carpenters helped build the war machine that finally defeated the Axis powers. They did more—an ambulance from Brooklyn Local 1204's 400 members contributed to the Red Cross; a new cafeteria steam table for the enlisted men's service club at Camp Lee, Virginia, a gift from Local 1534; the U. S. O. built by the voluntary labor of members of Bay Counties District Council. Members bought war bonds, some $30-million worth by mid-1943. When asked what his troops would appreciate most, General Douglas MacArthur said, "American cigarettes," and so, before the war was over, Brotherhood members provided approximately thirty million free union label cigarettes to the men and women overseas. What this simple gift meant was perhaps best expressed in a letter from Naval Chaplain Fred W. Marsh, who wrote in April 1945 from somewhere in the Pacific. "You will be interested to know that at least two cases (eighty cartons) of the cigarettes you sent to service men are going to men wounded in action. When these men leave the beaches they don't carry much, and to have all the cigarettes they want means a great deal to them. If you could see their smiles of appreciation when they take a pack—or two or three—you would feel well rewarded for your gift."

"Ever hear of Carpenters' Union, Local 162, San Mateo, California?" News columnist Elsie Robinson asked, early in the war. "Probably not—they're not seeking publicity. Defense time's too precious to spend in talking about themselves. Yet, in spite of the rush, they're managing to do something mighty interesting. Every week a selected batch of them . . . fifteen or so . . . drop in at a local hospital, peel off their coats, wait quietly while the Doc drains a pint of blood from each. Then, as quietly, go their way. . . . None of them talk about what they do and none will accept a cent. It isn't a big gesture to them. It's just their way of being 'regular' . . . of being American."

Building blood banks or building ships, carpenters were engaged in the war against fascism. In recognition of the carpenter contribution, one of the growing fleet of cargo ships was christened the SS *Peter J. McGuire* on Labor Day, 1942, and launched at the Richmond Yards, near San Francisco. In March, 1943, another— launched in Baltimore—was named after Santiago Iglesias, carpenter of Puerto Rico. When the Army needed construction workers for two Manhattan Engineer District projects, it turned to the labor movement. As *The Carpenter* later reported, "by reasons of its immensity and uniqueness and . . . new practices never before used . . ., it was necessary that Judge Robert Patterson, the Under Secretary of War, call in the leaders, including . . . our own General President. . . . They, in a great many instances, broke down conditions of long standing in order that the completion *on* schedule be not interfered with." The Brotherhood concentrated all its efforts on keeping the projects supplied with capable carpenters. Many local unions, district and state councils played an important part in recruiting men. When it was over, on August 8, 1945, Under-Secretary Patterson wrote Brotherhood President Hutcheson,

"Your assistance in recruiting skilled mechanics to help the Clinton and Hanford Projects was an important factor in rushing these projects to completion and making it possible to drop the first Atomic Bomb on Japan. I want to thank the officers and members of your organization for this contribution to Victory." And at the end of the war, Secretary of the Navy James Forrestal wrote: "Among the unions which have worked with the Navy to build our enormous chain of bases at home and abroad, your Union has been outstanding. Your members deserve to carry with them into peace, therefore, a special sense of pride in a great national achievement."

The war, among other things, meant change for the Brotherhood. By January, 1943, there were so many inquiries to the national office about the acceptance of women as members that the officers were constrained to reply: "It has been decided that women engaged in any industry or performing work coming under the jurisdiction of the United Brotherhood of Carpenters and Joiners of America and receiving the same pay as men are eligible to membership. They will be required to pay the same initiation fee, the same monthly dues and otherwise be governed by all of the provisions of the General Constitution and Laws of the United Brotherhood. They will also be entitled to all the rights, benefits and privileges of the Organization the same as any other member." Shortly after, Local 2759, Mattawa, Ontario, elected the first female recording secretary-treasurer of a local union in Ontario. Miss Isabel Regimbal was the one and only woman to hold such a position. Whether she was the first in the Brotherhood, the records do not show, but this was sufficiently new for *The Carpenter* to feature her picture.

The war, too, engendered a spectacular growth in Brotherhood membership, a rise from just under 320,000 in 1940 to over 600,000 by war's end. But the greatest change experienced by the union was in its relationship to government. True, the Brotherhood had some experience with such a relationship during World War I, enough so that Hutcheson, drawing on that experience, could suggest months before the outbreak of hostilities the setting up of a National War Labor Board. Nonetheless, the relationship would be far greater than that of World War I and would have more lasting consequences.

The day after Pearl Harbor, President Hutcheson telegraphed President Franklin D. Roosevelt:

> Heretofore I have opposed sending an expeditionary force overseas. Now that our country has been attacked it is the duty of every American to help in every way he can to supply and produce the necessary munitions of war so that we can speedily overcome our enemies and show them than we cannot be ruthlessly attacked without retaliating. There should not now be any need for Congress to give consideration to anti-strike legislation as I am sure that members of the various labor organizations regardless as to their affiliation will show their patriotism as real Americans by refraining from committing any act or taking any action that would in any way handicap or slow up the progress in preparing and manufacturing the necessary munitions of war and to that end I desire to offer for myself and the members of the Brotherhood our cooperation and service in any way that it may be needed.

Loyal cooperation entailed equality of sacrifice. From the first, the Brotherhood's leaders recognized—as did most of the carpenters—that some of the people's rights and prerogatives might have to be abridged in the interest of winning the war. But they also maintained that a three-way yardstick should be applied to every piece of legislation placing in escrow traditional freedoms of any or all groups of citizens. Before such a law was passed, or such steps taken, it should be determined beyond a possibility of a doubt that (1) it was absolutely necessary; (2) it was limited to duration only; and (3) it was arrived at through voluntary procedures, with those whose rights would be trampled on assenting.

"Free Labor Will Win," was the proud slogan of the labor movement. Implicit in this, of course, were the "voluntary procedures" of free collective bargaining. However, these were sharply modified by the exigencies of war, though the natural conflict between labor and management remained. As Joel Seidman noted in his study, *American Labor from Defense to Reconversion*, the war demanded an extraordinary degree of union-management co-operation. Wage disputes were less acute, especially in war production, since the government footed the bill and high wages would assure an adequate supply of labor in a period of a labor shortage. "With skilled labor and scarce raw materials the key factors, rather than monetary costs as in peacetime," Seidman observed, "and with the government present, as consumer or as wage and price regulator in every negotiation, a significant change in the collective bargaining relationship was inevitable."

Union security, however, persisted as a source of conflict, partly, as Seidman observed, "because it helped hold the unions together, while the strike weapon was given up and partly because it would influence the postwar strength, and therefore the postwar bargaining position of the parties." The Brotherhood was fully aware of this since the World War I solution—a freezing of union *and* open shops—proved inadequate and contributed to the serious weakening of the trade unions in the 1920s. The union wanted no part of the open shop. It insisted on the union shop, arguing that union security was even more essential in wartime than in peacetime when workers were free to walk off the job if conditions were not right.

The issue cropped up at a labor and management conference summoned by the President in the weeks following Pearl Harbor. The conferees agreed that there should be no strikes or lockouts for the duration of the war. But they deadlocked on the issue of union security. Industrialists demanded the World War I solution, a freezing of the status quo; the unionists insisted that a proposed wartime labor board be empowered to grant a union or closed shop where open shops had prevailed at the outbreak of the war.

The issue was left to the discretion of the War Labor Board, created by the President in January, 1942, with William H. Davis, a former patent attorney and chairman of the National Defense Mediation Board, as chairman. Though the Board declared the issue on the basis of individual cases throughout the war, it soon worked out an effective union security policy: the maintenance of union membership. This provided an individual employee with an escape period of 15 days, during which he could withdraw from the collective bargaining unit for the duration of the labor agreement.

"By and large," Frank F. Graham stated, "the maintenance of stable union membership makes for the maintenance of responsible union leadership and responsible union discipline, makes for keeping faithfully the terms of the contract, and provides a stable basis for union-management cooperation for more efficient production." Its wisdom was confirmed by labor's wartime record. In shipbuilding, for example, where 90 percent of those then employed had to be trained before taking on the job, carpenters contributed to the outstanding achievement—542 Liberty ships, 62 tankers, 5 ore-carriers, 62 long-range C-type ships, 55 cargo carriers for the British, 5 coastwise ships and 15 special type craft (8.09 deadweight tons)—delivered within one year, 1942. That year only five one-hundredths of one percent of war work was delayed because of strikes. "That record has never been equaled in this country," declared President Roosevelt.

War created the need for price and wage controls and the government agencies to regulate them. Labor had little to do with the Office of Price Administration, except as an active part of the President's hold-the-line constituency. But it was directly involved in wage stabilization. The Brotherhood and other building trades unions argued that a separate body, rather than an all-inclusive one, to handle wage stabilization for the crafts would be more effective. What they accomplished is a remarkable tribute to the Brotherhood's adherence to "voluntarism."

Conditions specific to the construction industry warranted special attention. There was a pressing need for orderly procedures in a chaotic and highly competitive industry, whose essential character was not profoundly changed by the war. Wage stabilization was crucial if labor shortages and unrest were to be averted. This problem was made more pressing by the rising cost of living and by the necessity of equalizing wage rates in isolated areas as well as populated areas, in order that an adequate supply of men could be guaranteed to those projects which were located far distant from a natural source of skilled mechanics.

Public pressures for a wage freeze continued to mount during the first months of the war. Pointing to a 12-percent rise in the cost of living, A. F. of L. economists argued that the rise had been even greater in most war industry centers. In addition, there had been no general or substantial wage increases while the OPA had been ineffective in holding down prices. Corporate net profits hit, in 1941, a $7,200,000,000 high, equaled only in the 1929 boom, while real wages had fallen, especially for those workers who had remained on the same job.

The Federation proposed voluntary pay allotments to divert a billion dollars of buying power to defense bonds. It also called for increased social security taxes to finance expanded benefits, increased income taxes over an income level essential to health and efficiency, higher corporation taxes to prevent profiteering, and rationing of scarce goods at reasonable prices. Democratic collective bargaining, the Federation insisted, had to be preserved to avoid the devastating impact on our war effort of any developing fascist-like regimentation.

Alarmed by the failure of measures aimed at inflation, President Roosevelt presented a seven-point program in his critical April 27, 1942 message to Congress. He stressed the need for wage stabilization, called for heavy taxes on profits, a $25,000 limit on incomes after taxes, strict price ceilings, rationing of scarce commodities, a reduction in farm prices to parity, curtailment of credit and installment buying, and called for large-scale voluntary war bond purchases.

During the week of May 10, President Roosevelt met with Hutcheson and the members of the executive board of the Building and Construction Trades Department of the A. F. of L. He proposed the stabilization of wages in the industry as of May 1, 1942. Hutcheson and his associates pointed out that the expiration dates of existing contracts were concentrated in the first half of the year, and many, as yet, had not been renewed. After discussion, an agreement was reached on May 22. The President established a Wage Stabilization Board, with four members each from employers, labor and the public, for the purpose of adjusting any wage rates which proved to be inadequate as of July 1 when building and construction wage rates were stabilized. Maurice A. Hutcheson, son of William L. Hutcheson, and a Brotherhood General Vice President, served as one of three alternate members.

The Wage Stabilization Board worked and worked well. Its decisions were generally accepted and strikes were avoided.

One of the consequences of the general wartime feeling of unity was an attempt at the amalgamation of the A. F of L. and the CIO. John L. Lewis instigated the move, and Big Bill Hutcheson backed it within the councils of the Federation. Both believed that labor unity would strengthen the war effort, the country itself. Hutcheson served on the A. F. of L. peace committee along with Dan Tobin of the Teamsters and Harry Bates of the Bricklayers. They met on December 2, 1942, with their CIO counterparts— Philip Murray, head of the CIO and the Steelworkers, R. J. Thomas of the Auto Workers, and Julius Emspak of the Electrical Workers. Both sides appeared to agree to hear and determine the disputed jurisdictional disputes and to establish joint action on all issues directed toward an intensified prosecution of the war, anti-labor legislation, organizing the unorganized.

But this initial effort disintegrated in the face of personal and institutional rivalries. Bad feelings rooted in the initial break-away of the CIO unions were exacerbated by continued raiding, boiling over in this instance when the CIO raided A. F. of L. unions at the Kaiser Shipyards in California. Dismayed, Hutcheson gave up hopes of immediate unification. He had, he said, come to the conclusion that there was no sincerity among the CIO representatives; that they did not ever intend to come into the Federation for the simple reason that the activities of some of them were subversive. Though he excepted Phil Murray, Hutcheson recognized that the bad feeling between Murray and Lewis would not be easily overcome. At Lewis's urging, the United Mine Workers withdrew from the CIO and in the spring of 1943 applied for re-admission to the A. F. of L. Hutcheson led the fight for the re-affiliation of the errant Miners, but it took three years to win. The mine union rejoined the Federation in January, 1946, but withdrew again shortly thereafter.

Inevitably, the strains of waging war were reflected within the country as a whole and within the workforce. Workers increasingly felt tight-jacketed by a rising cost of living, despite government attempts at holding the line on price increases and the limited relief on wages secured through the so-called Little-Steel formula. Based on a settlement between the Little Steel companies and the Steelworkers, the formula allowed up to a 15-percent wage increase (since 1941) to compensate for inflation. Grievances began to pile up, aggravated by a backlog of 17,000 undecided cases before the War Labor Board. "Workers, war-weary and fearful about their postwar future seem to be grabbing almost any excuse for a strike these days," a *Wall Street Journal* leader began in the summer of 1944. Man-days lost peaked in 1943 at 13.5-million as a result of work stoppages. Though WLB chairman Davis placed the loss in perspective by pointing out that there had been one year of work gained for every hour lost, Congress, noticeably irate over a series of strikes in the nation's coalfields, passed over Presidential veto the Smith-Connally Act. It empowered the President to: seize struck facilities; punish by fine or imprisonment a strike at a plant in the government's possession; require a 30-day cooling-off period following a strike notice; and prescribe that a strike vote be taken on the thirtieth day by the National Labor Relations Board.

As predicted, the Smith-Connally Act exacerbated matters. President Roosevelt seized the coal mines and the railroads; settlements were worked out at great cost in terms of social dislocation. Early in 1944, the President in his annual message to Congress proposed immediate passage of a National Service Act empowering the government to say who shall work, where and for how long. "Forced labor," *The Carpenter* declared, "is contrary to all concepts of democracy and Americanism. . . . As labor has often pointed out, there is a vast difference between doing one's duty toward one's country and being compelled to do something from which some other citizen will make profit." Terming the proposal unwarranted and unnecessary, the Brotherhood pledged its opposition to compulsory labor "to the bitter end." (Communists within the CIO, incidentally, supported the proposed labor draft.)

"With election day just around the corner," *The Carpenter* speculated, "it is not beyond the pale of possibility that politics, not production needs may be the motivating influence behind talk of a National Service Act." Even though President Roosevelt's proposal was not enacted, it—and the continued deterioration of wartime labor-management relations—prompted the Brotherhood's General Executive Board to take an unusual step. It approved, unanimously, a political statement, drafted by President Hutcheson:

> Every so often, a single year flares out historically as a turning point in human progress. 1944 seems destined to be such a year. Vast social and economic issues are coming to a focus. Long evaded realities must be faced. Just as this is the "year of decision" of our great and uncompleted war task, so the choice which the American people will make in the 1944 Presidential election will determine the shape and direction of our national economy for at least a generation. . . .
>
> It is my conviction that the New Deal Administration has shown itself incapable; that its methods and policies have, themselves, created new threats to our national economy more disquieting than those which we have been attempting to escape; that wage-earners have been victims of a cruel political deception in that our economy has been entrusted to visionaries. When war ends, the twelve million men and women in the armed forces want to return to honest-to-God jobs. . . .
>
> Labor demands of both national and political parties that the candidates shall have the ability and their platforms the assurance of a progressive leadership to the end that the nation shall have
>
> 1. The preservation of free enterprise.
> 2. The abatement of bureaucracy.
> 3. The halt of paternalism.
> 4. The creation of post-war jobs through private industry.
> 5. The maintenance of labor's social gains.
> 6. The protection of our national interest. . . .
>
> The maintenance and elevation of the American standard of living is inextricably woven in the foregoing fundamentals. Our American economy is geared to the sustained purchasing power of our wage and salary earners. Only by this preservation can we avoid a short-sighted post-war assault upon the American wage structure, as was experienced following World War I. . . .

Though ostensibly addressed to politicians of both parties, the statement leaned toward Republican endorsement. Brotherhood President Hutcheson was considered, not seriously as it turned out, a possible Republican Vice-Presidential candidate. The Brotherhood, in 1944, adhered to its traditional non-involvement stance. Yet, the statement was an indication that it was prepared to intervene politically should issues arise of sufficient gravity to organized labor.

By mid-1943, the Brotherhood began considering the post-war tasks confronting the country. As Hutcheson put it, "The transition from a state-directed war economy to peacetime private enterprise will require vast economic readjustments. It was essential that we clarify the afterwar relationship between industry and government."

Recognizing that the needs of war required a controlled economy, Hutcheson argued that, before the war ended, to avoid confusion of purpose and thought in the days ahead, it was desirable to re-state fundamental principles.

"The after-war years," Hutcheson wrote, "will impose upon the people of America not only the reconstitution of our own domestic economy, but also a vast program of assistance in the reconstruction of the war-ravaged nations of the world. . . . Obviously, the transition from government planning to a private economy cannot be made abruptly. But that this restoration should be achieved with the minimum of necessary delay, when war ends, is the deep conviction of all those who have faith in the validity of our traditional economical way of life."

As the war came to an end, labor urged the restoration of free collective bargaining sixty days after the surrender of the Axis powers. When Germany was knocked out of the war, *The Carpenter* declared: "If wages are raised now, post-war purchasing power will be high enough to keep our post-war economy at a high peak." When Japan surrendered, *The Carpenter* remarked in the midst of VJ-Day celebrations that "four years of super-human effort" defeated the enemy. "It took heartache and backache and pain to do the job—the heartache of those who saw loved ones go off to war, the backache of those who spent long hours on production jobs, and the pain of those who faced the enemy—but with God's help victory has been achieved."

Yet, the Brotherhood's publication warned, there remain "deadly enemies at home. . . . A newspaper chain in recent weeks has exposed the machinations of a nationalist group that hopes to emulate Hitler by capitalizing on Greed, Intolerance, and Hate.

The Communist Party reorganizes behind barred doors to plot new ways and means of infiltrating labor and other basic groups. Several bills aimed at hamstringing labor appear in Congress. And behind all these moves Hate, or Greed, or Intolerance (or all three) provides the motivating force. . . .

"Communism and Fascism will propagandize and plot, but there is one sure-fire antidote. Give every American a chance to have and hold a job commensurate with his abilities and his ambitions. Give him a chance to rear his family in decent and self-respecting surroundings. Give him a chance to educate his children to the full measure of their promise. Give him a chance to grow and expand and enrich his own life and the lives of his neighbors. Give him a chance to shape and fulfill his own destiny. Give him a chance to face the future with confidence. When we have assured him of these things we need have no fear of Fascism or Communism or Hate or Greed or Intolerance."

Nothing will be achieved, *The Carpenter* added, "by opportunists organizing employer groups to smash organized labor. Neither will they be achieved by harum-scarum unionism which has its nose buried deeper in politics and foreign isms than in promoting the welfare of the members it is supposed to represent. . . .

"The cost of the war in suffering, human lives, and money has been staggering. If it taught us nothing else it should have taught us that with unity we can achieve any goal we set for ourselves. Let us, therefore, attack the problems of peace with the same spirit of cooperation, unity, and sincerity with which we transformed a relatively unarmed America into the greatest fighting force in the world's history in a couple of short years."

Clearly, in morale and spirit, not to mention strength, the Brotherhood was ready to confront the travails of peace.

X

THE PROMISE OF LABOR PEACE

The war ended. The marines and the sea-bees, the soldiers and sailors came home. The country had a new President, a scrappy fellow from Missouri, Harry S. Truman, and some folk wondered if he was up to the job. Europe was ravaged by war. An atomic bomb mushroomed over Hiroshima and Nagasaki. The Soviets swallowed Eastern Europe and millions were sent to the Gulag Archipelago, prisoners of the seemingly endless totalitarian night.

Our country emerged from the war an awkward giant, a new world power with heretofore unimagined responsibilities. The world needed re-building and carpenters were ready to shoulder their share of the work. The Brotherhood pledged the same unqualified support to the winning of the peace that it devoted to the winning of the war. To fellow workers in other nations, it extended the hand of brotherhood. As a General Executive Board Declaration noted: "Under the totalitarian heel, workers felt the ruthless lash of domination. Yet from the ranks of labor sprang the backbone of the resistance movement. Those union leaders who were not butchered outright took up the cudgels against the foe. . . . Democracy will never be restored fully to these nations until the free trade unions are re-built."

Elated by the sudden release of energies pent up by the exigencies of war, Americans were also fearful and worried lest boom become bust and progress become reaction. There were fears of massive unemployment, of veterans selling pencils on street-corners. Charles G. Bolte, a veteran who had lost a leg in North Africa, cautioned in prestigious *Harper's Magazine* that "in the twelve million veterans who are disillusioned with the promise of democracy there lies a grave potential danger."

Carpenters had more faith in those who had fought for their country. Veterans were welcomed back. Journeymen serving their country had remained members-in-good-standing without having to pay dues while in service. Young men who went off to fight returning too old to finish apprenticeships under the rules found their slots still open as the union waived age limits. The Brotherhood also made sure that the G.I. Bill educational features were not limited solely to the college-bound. Joint labor-management committees were recognized as appropriate training institutions so that veterans could get needed job training.

While carpenters held steadfast to their faith in their country and the returning GIs, economic uncertainties clearly underscored fears of renewed union-busting on the pattern of the open-shop drives of the 1920s. A flood of anti-union measures filled Congressional hoppers. So-called "Right-to-Work" measures were enacted in a goodly number of state legislatures, especially in states where trade unionism was weak. President Truman pleaded for a continuance of the no-strike pledge and sought in vain to hold down prices though wages remained "frozen." As Willard Wirtz, then chairman of the National Wage Stabilization Board, described the situation; "Labor cannot be expected to pay decontrolled prices with controlled wages." The whole set-up, claimed *The Carpenter*, "was created to guarantee profits to the manufacturers and distributors and at the same time to hold down wages as closely as possible to an artificial "line." It was a situation that could lead to one result only—another wave of industrial unrest."

Over four-and-a-half million workers marched on picket lines in 1946, a half million more than the previous peak, in fateful 1919. One hundred and thirteen million man-days of labor were lost, three times as many as 1945 and the largest number in our history. Strikes halted production in coal, auto, electric, steel and in the Pacific northwest where 60,000 lumber and sawmill workers struck for a wage increase commensurate with prevailing conditions. Maritime and rail transportation ground to a halt. When coal miners struck, President Truman seized the mines under wartime powers until a settlement was reached.

The post-war strike wave underscored a point raised by the October, 1946, *Carpenter*: "If the government cannot institute and maintain a healthy relationship between prices and wages, then government control must go." A General Executive Board statement noted, "our employers and union representatives . . . have proven they are fully capable of sitting down together and reaching an agreement satisfactory to both. . . . These men who have made the construction industry their life work . . . understand each other's problems far better than any bureaucrats, no matter how sincere. . . ." Wartime controls were removed in November, 1946, and free collective bargaining resumed—but not without opposition.

In the California redwoods, 5,000 Brotherhood members battled powerful forest "barons" for elemental trade union rights. On January 14, 1946, they struck for modest wage gains in line with those won by Pine and Fir workers in Oregon and Washington. Emboldened by tax carryovers that made it profitable "to take a strike," the redwood barons simply shut down their mills. Workers were evicted from company-owned houses. When the tax boon thinned out at the end of the year, the mills were re-opened with scab labor. Deputy sheriffs were mobilized to enlarge the thin trickle of scab lumber. Vice President Maurice Hutcheson flew to the coast in a vain effort to negotiate a settlement. The Bay Counties District Council voted a contribution of $3 a member, roughly a total of $60,000, to the strikers. The Northwest Council of Lumber and Sawmill Workers raised a $1-per-member-per-month for the embattled Redwood workers. The importance of the union label was again stressed throughout the Brotherhood. Redwood lumber produced under fair conditions, carpenters were reminded, would bear the "clearance" label, AFL 8. All else was a product of unfair mills.

Slowly, the determined Redwood workers broke the back of anti-union forces centered around the nine major redwood producers. In February, 1947, after 13 months of bitter struggle, came the first break, a contract with one of the largest opeators in the industry, Hammond Lumber Company. The new agreement provided a minimum wage of $1.20 an hour, a straight-across-the-board increase of thirty-five cents an hour in all classifications above the minimum. But the strike dragged on, lasting for two years and three months. In April, 1948, the Redwood workers voted to terminate the strike. By then, only some six or seven firms out of the hundred-odd originally struck were still involved.

While the Redwood workers may not have obtained all of their objectives, *The Carpenter* noted, "they did clean up what was a very nasty situation in the Redwoods. . . . the Redwood territory is a far different place from what it was three years ago. For one thing, wages are now $1.40 as compared to the 82½¢ that prevailed prior to the strike. For another thing, the monopoly of the Redwood barons has been shaken. Scores of new companies moved into the territory during the strike. These new firms are all under agreement with the Union. They are all paying union wages and meeting union conditions. It is estimated that there are something like 175 Union Shop agreements in effect in the Redwood territory at the present time. The number of Local Unions in the area has grown from twenty-six before the strike to thirty-nine at the present time. Membership increased by about eighty percent. Considering all these things the long struggle of Redwood workers will pay dividends for years to come."

Unions emerged from the war and the post-war wave of strike turbulence stronger than ever before. The Brotherhood, for example, reached the 800,000-member mark in 1951, becoming the fourth largest union in America. The A. F. of L. membership passed the 9-million mark that year, and the CIO, which had expelled its Communist-led unions in 1948, counted 4.1-million members.

Growth, however, was achieved in the face of a renewed opposition. Post-war labor-management conflict produced a political reaction, a rise in animosity toward what many perceived as "big labor." Encouraged by anti-union employers, sentiment for restrictive legislation mounted. As George Meany, then Secretary-Treasurer of the A. F. of L. graphically summed up the situation:

No company sluggers this time; no sawed-off shotguns or teargas. No, this time the means used is going to be more subtle. In the interest of industrial peace we must have just a little bit of compulsory legislation for labor. Just a little compulsory arbitration at first. Then a little compulsory work legislation. Then maybe we will have a little revival of government by injunction. Then, perhaps, a little bit of the old conspiracy doctrine, under which any worker who suggests to another worker that they both cease work would be liable for monetary damages and perhaps a jail sentence on a criminal charge.

Somehow, it was widely believed, legislation would be a cure-all. Were this true, Brotherhood President Hutcheson told President Truman at a 1946 meeting, the world might be a happier place. Drawing on his half-century experience in the labor movement, Hutcheson added, "I have seen ideas, patterns, and theories come and go. But in all this time I have never seen a sound concept of labor relations incorporated into the American way of life but what that concept was based on the fundamental premise that men must be free to work or not to work, to do business or not to do business, to accept or not to accept chances that the vagaries of ever-changing conditions present."

Unhappily, Congress was not ready to listen to Hutcheson or other union spokesmen. The Taft-Hartley Act, named after its sponsors Senator Robert A. Taft and Representative Fred A. Hartley, was enacted by Congress in June, 1947. Though vetoed by President Truman, it was passed over his objections and became the law of the land.

Taft-Hartley, as Richard Gray, president of the A. F. of L. Building Trades Department, told delegates to the Brotherhood's 1950 convention, hit harder at building and construction trades unions than at any other segment of organized labor. The first union hit was the Brotherhood in a case that outlawed customary practices of contracting and job referral. In the Hamm Drayage and Atkinson-Jones cases the NLRB held that an agreement, to be legal, must be made only after a job had started and enough men hired to determine an appropriate bargaining unit. "Most construction jobs," Gray noted, "would be finished long before the union could go through all the red tape and complicated procedure of securing certification. . . . It is thus virtually impossible for us to bargain within the provisions of the law, for our members."

The law's most onerous provision, perhaps, was the notorious Section 14 (b), which permits states to pass laws forbidding union shop contracts, or what amounts to compulsory open shops. Nineteen states took advantage of this invitation to turn back the clock.

George Meany, at the Brotherhood's 1954 convention, described what happened, as a consequence of Taft-Hartley, at the Bull Shoals Dam. Started in the summer of 1947, the dam was built by a notorious anti-union contractor. "We got the men in the union," Meany told the carpenter delegates, "got union men on the job. We tried to talk to the company to bargain collectively, and we went through five years of NLRB procedure under the Taft-Hartley Act with every obstacle that the employer could use in the law placed in our way. During the five years of procedure, including court cases, regional director decisions, NLRB decisions, every type of decision, every single decision starting in the summer of 1947 right down to 1952 was won by the union. We won every single decision under the law, and in September of 1952 the President of the United States went down and dedicated that dam and put it into operation and there hadn't been any collective bargaining on the job or any recognition of the union."

Yet, as *The Carpenter* noted in its August, 1947, editorial, "all this does not change the fact that the Bill is now law. We have to live with it, so we might as well look it squarely in the eye and make our plans accordingly."

That look entailed a renewed commitment. As *The Carpenter* put it, "We must have faith in our unions. We must give them the best that is in us." And that carpenters did as The Brotherhood held out against Taft-Hartley forays. In June, 1948, for example, carpenters voted ninety-nine percent in favor of the union shop in a series of Western Pennsylvania elections. Pile drivers, also members of the Brotherhood, voted 100 percent. It was a remarkable demonstration of loyalty and union-mindedness.

At the A. F. of L.'s sixty-sixth convention, the Brotherhood's delegation joined with the rest of the delegates in a unanimous answer to the challenge of the predatory and vested interests which invented and fostered and put over the Taft-Hartley Act. Without a dissenting vote, the convention adopted a proposal for the immediate establishment of a political arm, Labor's Educational and Political League. "The vested interests can be stopped," Peter E. Terzick, then assistant editor of *The Carpenter*, commented in a special editorial a few months later, "but they can be stopped in only one way—through the ballot box." For the 1948 elections, *The Carpenter* carried, for the first time, the voting record of every Congressman and every Senator on many bills which were of vital interest to labor. Members were urged to study the record of the incumbents and of their opponents. "That is the surest way of knowing whether they were for you or against you." The General Executive Board urged Brotherhood local unions and district councils to take an active part in the League and backed its exhortation with a $100,000 voluntary contribution.

Political action, of course, was not the Brotherhood's sole response to the challenges workers faced in the post-war world. In the courts, the Brotherhood won two key victories which helped unions survive under Taft-Hartley. Chattanooga Local 74 sought to organize, unsuccessfully, some workers engaged in laying of linoleum in homes and newly constructed houses. It picketed the company with "Don't Patronize" signs and the employer filed suit under the antiboycott provisions of the Taft-Hartley Act. The Tennessee courts held, however, that such picketing was not for illegal purposes but for purposes beneficial to the union, and that such picketing was protected by the Constitution. In Colorado, union craftsmen employed on a Denver construction project refused to work with non-union men. The employer filed "unfair labor" charges, seeking an injunction on the grounds that the unions were violating the anti-boycott sections of Taft-Hartley. A Colorado judge denied the injunction on the grounds that Taft-Hartley could not be applied to *local* construction because the firm was not actually engaged in interstate commerce despite its handling of materials

In late 1940s Brotherhood General Executive Board faced new challenges. Left to right are: Roland Adams, 4th District; Harry Schwarzer, 3rd District; William Kelley, 2nd District; Frank Duffy, general secretary; William L. Hutcheson, General President; Maurice A, Hutcheson, First General Vice President; S. P. Meadows, General Treasurer; Arthur Martel, Canadian District; and Robert E. Roberts, 5th District board member.

manufactured in other states. The judge further ruled that posting an Unfair List was lawful, protected by the "free speech" provisions of the Act.

The Brotherhood also strengthened itself by urging more and more semi-beneficial locals to become fully beneficial so that all members could become "full citizens" with all the rights of membership. (In 1948, the Brotherhood had 541 semi-beneficial locals with 134,386 members; by 1953, the number of such locals was down to 185 with 41,000 members.) In 1948, the Brotherhood doubled its maximum death benefit from $300 to $600 and increased the wife's funeral benefit by 100 percent—both at the slight increase per capita of 25 cents. "A rare bargain," declared the G.E.B. Accounting and administrative procedures were streamlined at the international office to better serve the members.

The twenty-fifth convention, in 1946, called for the establishment of an apprenticeship committee to set up standards for training. Under the chairmanship of Maurice Hutcheson, the committee did yeoman's work in drawing up a comprehensive manual.* The first units were ready for the 1950 convention and twelve units were off the press by 1954. At the close of 1953, 35,985 members were registered on the Brotherhood's books as apprentices and during the preceeding four years, 13,799 young men were granted journeymen's certificates by the General Office. United States Department of Labor statistics showed the Brotherhood to be by far the most active in apprenticeship training in the construction trades. With justifiable pride, Maurice Hutcheson was able to inform the 1954 convention that the apprenticeship training program was on a sound footing and in gear with the times. However, he also warned of neglect at the local level in establishing sound programs. "The search for ways and means of improving and making more effective the apprenticeship training program is a never-ending process at both the local and international level."

With the outbreak of the Korean War, the Brotherhood once again faced the problem of working within a maze of wartime

---

* Members of that committee were: Asgar Andrup, Chicago; Carl Schwarzer, Cleveland; Leo Gable, Long Beach; and John McMahon, Buffalo.

regulations. New programs were developed. In 1950, the New York District Council negotiated a three-percent payroll tax contribution from employers to establish a Carpenters Welfare Fund "for the protection of the membership when they are unable to work due to illness or accidents not incurred on the job." At the 1954 convention, President Maurice Hutcheson appointed the Brotherhood's first Health and Welfare Committee, which urged that all constituent bodies seek to establish health and welfare programs. Such programs, with provisions for health care, hospitalization benefits, disability payments were one of the largest contributions to the overall welfare of working people and their families that the labor movement in the United States was able to make within the past twenty years. Since the difficulties and problems to be met in setting up a health and welfare program are many and complicated, the Committee also warned that no Local or District Council should participate in the creation of such a program without first securing all the information available to it from those of the Brotherhood who had already gone through the problem. With this in mind, the General Officers were urged to undertake collection of all the relevant data concerning Brotherhood experience with health and welfare benefits. It was also recommended that the Brotherhood create a Department of Health and Welfare.

To help make the Carpenter's Union more effective, a series of regional conferences was held in 1953. One of the recommendations that came out of these down-to-earth sessions was one for a Department of Organization. In March, 1954, Frank M. Chapman was appointed Director of Organization. Later in the year, Chapman put on a second hat when he succeeded Spurgeon P. Meadows as General Treasurer.

Chapman was a natural choice as the Brotherhood's top organizer. A sawmill worker from Snoqualmie, Washington, he became a key figure in the organization of the Northwest lumber industry. During the long and bitter strike for recognition, he was hounded by the National Guard and beaten by the special police. After fourteen years as a general representative in organizing work, he became four-state co-ordinator for Brotherhood activities in the

Northwest, a post he held for four years until he was called to Indianapolis for the new position.

One reason for the creation of the new post was the need for innovation in this key area. For example, jurisdictional conflicts and raids by so-called independent unions in the highway and heavy construction fields cried out for new approaches from organized labor. In late 1954, the Brotherhood, the Laborers, Teamsters and Operating Engineers decided to co-ordinate their efforts to organize the industry. President Eisenhower had asked for a vast expansion of highway building, and the various states were contemplating additional road construction. A new technology had evolved in highway construction, requiring vast quantities of carpentry. The new superhighways the nation had to build contained many bridges, overpasses, underpasses and cloverleafs, all of which entailed considerable form work. By co-ordinating their efforts through a joint committee, the four unions aimed at protecting their respective jurisdictions and at promoting jobs for their members.

The years that followed the end of World War II took their inevitable toll. Frank Duffy, beloved of carpenters all across the land, retired in 1948 after 47 years of dedicated service. "You and I have been old friends," he wrote in his letter of resignation to President Hutcheson, "chums and pals for a long time and now I feel I can say with pride that we have been a great team. . . . None better. Let us remain so the balance of our lives." Duffy died at age 94 in 1955.

At the December 11, 1951 General Executive Board meeting, William L. Hutcheson tendered his resignation as President of the Brotherhood. "Having served our Brotherhood for many years," he wrote, always to the point, "I have come to the conclusion that it is advisable to step aside. . . ." In doing so, he added, "I want to say . . . that among the many thousand members we have I do not know of any group that could be selected that would be better qualified from experience and knowledge of the working of our organization than those of you who constitute the General Executive Board members, and I want to express to you, and through you to

Maurice A. Hutcheson (right), new president of the Brotherhood, enjoys a meeting with A. F. of L. President William Green (center) and U. S. Secretary of Labor James P. Mitchell.

the members of the Brotherhood my deep and sincere appreciation for the help, support and assistance that you and they gave me during my years of service."

Big Bill stepped down after 36 years of service as President of the Brotherhood. He remained in the service of the Brotherhood as a vice president of the A. F. of L. until his resignation from that post in 1953 and as President Emeritus of the Brotherhood until his death later that year.

Maurice A. Hutcheson, First General Vice President and Big Bill's oldest son, succeeded in accordance with the Brotherhood's constitution. Born on May 7, 1897, Maurice, as the son of a working carpenter, was expected to work and carry his share of the family's burdens. He peddled the *Detroit Free Press* on the streets of Saginaw as a schoolboy. He accompanied his father to the elder Hutcheson's first convention in 1910. When the family moved to Indianapolis in 1913 after his father's election as a Vice President, Maurice clerked in the union's bookkeeping department. On his 17th birthday, he joined Indianapolis Local 75 as an apprentice. By the time he was about to finish his apprenticeship, the United States was engaged in World War I. Young Maurice enlisted in the Navy, serving two years before returning home to pick up his tools as a journeyman carpenter.

Seized by a youthful wanderlust, never fully satisfied by his Navy stint, Maurice worked at dockbuilding in New York, shipbuilding in Brooklyn, and at general carpentry and mill work in Youngstown, Cleveland and many other cities around the country. In 1928, he was appointed a General Representative, frequently serving as an auditor because of his intimate knowledge of the union's bookkeeping practices and procedures. He visited many local unions in the course of his work, becoming familiar with the broad spectrum of the Brotherhood's membership and its interests. When First General Vice President George Lakey died in 1938, Maurice was the unanimous choice of the General Officers and General Executive Board to fill that spot. Frank Duffy enjoyed recounting how Big Bill "hit the ceiling" when Duffy first recommended Maurice. According to Duffy, Big Bill said, "Nothing doing, that is out of the question. If I do that and it is approved by the General Executive Board then they will say it is a Hutcheson family affair." Duffy's reply apparently sufficed: "Well," he said, "they say that anyhow."

Reserved in manner, more introspective than most labor leaders, Maurice was an enthusiastic reader in social science, history and politics. An able administrator, he was an effective troubleshooter, whether overseeing the organization of the Northwest lumber and sawmill industry or resolving conflicts within troubled district councils or local unions. He guided the apprenticeship committee's work to a fruitful conclusion. Aware of the growing complexities of organized labor in an age of rapid change, he not only kept abreast himself but organized the services of the Brotherhood to inform others. One pet project, for example, was the "Current Information" bulletin through which the General Office endeavored to keep all key officers informed of the latest developments in labor legislation, government directives and all matters affecting the construction industry. He was one of nine trade unionists to visit wartorn Europe in the spring of 1945, returning to report on the "last gasp" of Nazism. "And if I live to a thousand years I will never forget the things I saw," he declared. His insight into the nature of totalitarianism, reinforced by his European tour, went deeper than most for he was among the first to see that a democratic labor movement not only could make a contribution to the economic recovery of Europe but would serve in the forefront of the struggle against violent nationalism and Communist totalitarianism.

Maurice A. Hutcheson's qualities of leadership were severely tested in the period that followed his becoming President of the Brotherhood. William Green and Philip Murray died within a few days of each other in 1952. George Meany, Secretary-Treasurer of the A. F. of L., became President of the Federation. Walter P. Reuther, President of the United Auto Workers, became head of the CIO. Explorations of the possibilities of unification were begun. But the negotiations for a no-raiding agreement between A. F. of L. and CIO unions precipitated a crisis over jurisdiction and the Carpenters, the first time ever, walked out of the American Federation of Labor.

Sam Gompers once remarked that the question of jurisdiction was "beyond doubt the greatest problem, the greatest danger which, above all, threatens not only the success but the very existence of the American Federation of Labor." Yet, as John T. Dunlop, a noted expert in the field, pointed out to the delegates at the Brotherhood's 1954 convention, jurisdictional disputes were in some ways a blessing. They arise, he added, in part from the system of sub-contracting, as a product of technological progress, as a consequence of democratic processes within unions and from the diversity in local situations throughout this great land. You could not, Dunlop suggested, do away with jurisdictional disputes without doing irreparable harm to freedom of enterprise, progress, democracy itself.

The problem was not to eliminate disputes so much as to how best resolve them so as to enhance economic health, progress and democracy. Prior to the Wagner Act, as Dunlop pointed out, jurisdiction was within the provenance of the A. F. of L. In guaranteeing worker rights to representation and to free collective bargaining, the Act, however, put the government in the picture. NLRB was empowered to designate bargaining units and the choice of individual workers as expressed through majority vote determined affiliation rather than jurisdiction as spelled out by the A. F. of L.

Taft-Hartley and the so-called right-to-work laws made it clear that a strong gale of anti-unionism was blowing across the nation. When the Taft-Hartley Act was passed, the G.E.B. report to the 1950 convention stated that it was readily apparent that several provisions contained in the new law would restrict the Building and Construction Trades Department from rendering decisions on disputes that occurred among the different crafts. In sum, a prudent labor movement had best look to its defenses. Or, as Dunlop phrased it, "Either this industry solves its jurisdictional problems within its own family or the government will."

To forestall this eventuality, the Building and Construction Trades and the industry created, in 1948, the National Joint Board for the Settlement of Jurisdictional Disputes with John T. Dunlop as chairman. M. A. Hutcheson served as a member of the Joint Board. That the Joint Board made a good start is clearly evident. In its first year of operation, some 213 work stoppages over jurisdiction were successfully resolved. Within its first year under Taft-Hartley, some 73 cases involving jurisdiction were filed with the NLRB. The operation of the Joint Board made it unnecessary, except in one instance, for the NLRB to hold hearings. Subsequently, it became standard practice for regional NLRB officers to refer charging parties to the Board of Trustees of the Joint Board.

However, the Joint Board could do little or nothing about membership-poaching by unions outside the Building and Construction Trades. When the International Alliance of Theatrical and Stage Employees (IATSE), for example, moved in on the jurisdiction of Brotherhood's Hollywood Local 946, 2,200 Brotherhood members had to hit the street. The motion picture industry spent $7,000,000 and imported goons in an attempt to break the strike. The industry put pressure on Washington and the A. F. of L. to end the strike. The Federation Executive Council appointed a three-man commission to study and rule on the dispute. Its ruling was ambiguous. The commission then handed down an interpretation which was spurned by IATSE. The studio carpenters were discharged, turning a strike into a lock-out.

Such developments rankled so much that when the Federation and the CIO worked out the no-raiding agreement of 1953, William Hutcheson insisted, at the August 11, 1953 Council meeting considering the no-raid agreement, that the Federation put its own house in order first. When the council refused to consider his request, he left the meeting. On August 12, General President Maurice A. Hutcheson submitted to the Federation a letter of withdrawal on behalf of the Brotherhood. It did not withdraw lightly. The Federation, declared the G.E.B., had failed to recognize and remedy the situation that threatened to lead to complete chaos.

The situation referred to by the G.E.B. was detailed in a 1950–1952 survey which revealed that for over six years, section hands had been building roundhouses, chemical workers had erected gas plants and, in one instance, an A. F. of L. railroad union performed $300,000,000 worth of construction work. "Are carpenters," the Brotherhood asked, "to be expected to stand in Unemployment Insurance lines while section hands erect warehouses and chemical workers gas plants?"

"One need only to look about and ascertain the situation in which organized labor now finds itself," declared a report of the Building and Construction Trades Council. "For example, today we have a miner's union with bargaining rights over all employees in a shirt-waist making concern. We have long-shoremen representing employes in a candy making concern. We have chemical workers representing textile workers, and textile workers representing jewelry workers.

"We have now reached the point where many internationals feel obligated to go out and organize and obtain NLRB certification regardless of charter rights and their own constitutional jurisdictional provisions.

"Boiled down, it is a race to see who gets there first and obtains NLRB certification. Such a situation, in our opinion, amounts to outright surrender to a Governmental Board of the basic and inherent authority and power vested in the American Federation of Labor. No longer does our A. F. of L. Executive Council decide with authority which international has jurisdiction according to its AFL-granted charter—indeed not, these decisions now rest with a politically appointed governmental board."

The Brotherhood had no desire to impede the unification of the A. F. of L. and the CIO. M. A. Hutcheson remarked of the CIO, "at least they do not raid one another, but there are hundreds of cases of A. F. of L. unions raiding A. F. of L. unions." In view of this situation, he added, "it appears somewhat ludicrous to us that the Federation should be worrying about a no-raiding pact with the CIO while its own house remained in such disorder." The Brotherhood backed a remedy proposed by the Building and Construction Trades Department for bringing orderly procedure into the jurisdictional picture and returning to the Federation the responsibility for handling jurisdictional matters instead of having them kicked around by governmental agencies. The proposal entailed nothing more complicated than recognizing the seriousness of the jurisdictional problem, analyzing it as completely as possible, and, finally, setting up an impartial umpire to make jurisdictional decisions.

Ironically, the Brotherhood was cast in the role of an anti-merger dragon while the A. F. of L. was cast as St. George. In fact, the Brotherhood was involved in only fourteen out of 694 intra-A. F. of L. raiding cases. The desire to eliminate raiding was the very reason why the United Brotherhood of Carpenters left the Federation. Until the Federation adopted a more realistic attitude the United Brotherhood would have to go it alone. They had no intention of encroaching on anyone's jurisdiction, and by the same token they did not intend to let anyone encroach on theirs. They considered themselves still a part of the labor movement.

No one, in truth, wanted to see the break-up of the labor

movement. Harry Bates, president of the Bricklayers, acted promptly to bring the heads of the A. F. of L. and the Brotherhood together. General President Hutcheson, First General Vice President John R. Stevenson, Second Vice President O. Wm. Blaier, General Executive Board Members Charles Johnson, Jr., and Raleigh Rajoppi met with an A. F. of L. committee consisting of Meany, Secretary-Treasurer William Schnitzler, Bates, Daniel Tracy and W. C. Doherty. It was agreed that something would be done about raiding and that the Brotherhood would return to the Federation in time to send delegates to the Federation's 72nd convention in September, 1953.

There the efforts of the Brotherhood bore fruit. The convention unanimously approved the recommendation advanced by the Building and Construction Trades Department for setting up a special committee to study the overall jurisdictional problem and to recommend a workable solution. Had the A. F. of L. Council so acted, no walkout would have ensued.

In the spring of 1954, representatives from at least 100 A. F. of L. affiliates met in Chicago at a special conference called to consider a no-raid plan submitted by the special committee. The plan applied only to those organizations formally adopting it, and thereby agreeing to submit jurisdictional differences with other organizations to mediation, once direct negotiations proved fruitless, and to binding arbitration if such a step became necessary.

Meanwhile, the Brotherhood and the Machinists, in George Meany's words "set an example" for the labor movement in the voluntary resolution of jurisdictional disputes. On September 18, 1954, General President Maurice A. Hutcheson, for the Carpenters, and Al. J. Hayes, President of the IAM, signed a negotiated agreement that concluded the oldest and thorniest jurisdictional dispute in the history of labor, the 40-year quarrel over the installation of machinery.* Millwrights were acknowledged "car-

---

* Both unions acknowledged the invaluable contribution of the two advisors— John T. Dunlop, Harvard professor and Joint Board chariman, and Father William J. Kelley, a top-flight arbitrator for New York. (Dunlop was chosen by the Carpenters; Kelley, by the Machinists.) The negotiations were conducted by: M. A. Hutcheson, General President; O. Wm. Blaier; R. E. Roberts and Raleigh

*A. F. of L. and CIO merger in 1955 realizes P. J. McGuire's dream
of a united labor movement. George Meany and Walter P. Reuther
raise clasped hands to celebrate unity.*

Rajoppi for the Brotherhood and A. J. Hayes, Executive President; Eric Peterson,
P. L. Siemiller and Elmer E. Walker for the IAM.

penters;" but the lines between the crafts were more clearly delineated. In breweries, for example, millwrights retained jurisdiction over washers, pasteurizers and packaging machines, while machinists handled fillers, crowners, double seamers, and labelers along with the conveyors furnished with those machines.

Organized labor clearly was in a mood to handle its own problems without outside or government interference. As Meany said of the Carpenters'-Machinists' agreement, "They took it upon themselves to try and settle their own quarrel—and to me that is the best method of all." In that spirit, the A. F. of L. and the CIO came together in December, 1955.

Two years earler, the G.E.B. had unanimously gone on record as favoring any and all moves designed to unify the labor movement so long as such moves guaranteed the jurisdictional integrity of all parties concerned. In February, 1955, the Brotherhood approved the merger agreement thrashed out between the A. F. of L. and the CIO.

"Twenty years of mutually-destructive struggle," declared General President Hutcheson at the time of the merger, "will be brought to a close. The split in labor has been a costly one for American workers. Time and money and effort that could have and would have been devoted to improving wages and working conditions were spent in inter-union struggles for survival. A united labor movement has been one of the most pressing needs for the past 20 years.

"Will the merger be a cure-all? I wish I could say yes, but cold facts say otherwise. The merger agreement makes an honest effort to bring orderly procedures to bear on jurisdictional matters. It is a step in the right direction. It does not automatically solve the problems of dualism, but it does give all unions an opportunity to settle their differences by peaceful means, if they are willing and sincere. . . .

"We have built solidly and well. We can stand on our own two feet—forever if need be. But we do extend the hand of friendship to all those who want to share in the progress we have already made and the greater progress we are capable of making in the future."

XI

BROTHERHOOD EXPANDED

"These are times for prudence and calm deliberation," Maurice Hutcheson declared at the 1958 Brotherhood convention. Perplexing and precarious were the words he chose to describe the years that followed the merger of the A. F. of L. and the CIO in 1955.

"Throughout the world there is apprehension," Hutcheson said. "In the United States there is uneasiness as we scan the future. Business looks at our economy with some optimism, but also with watchful wariness. The entire labor movement is faced with unprecedented challenges from within and without."

Carpenters had decided in referendum to move the international headquarters from Indianapolis to the nation's capital. Some of the unease felt by the Brotherhood's leaders may have stemmed from the proposed move, for Indianapolis had been the home of the union for over a half-century. Other forces, however, were at work.

"I must admit that I considered that proposition with reluctance," John R. Stevenson, the Brotherhood's First General Vice President, once said, "but something happened in the State of Indiana that caused me to desire to get out of there as fast as I could. They passed the right-to-work law. That kind of disturbed me and because it disturbed me it disturbed my family, and after voting for nearly forty years as a Republican, I kicked over the traces and voted straight Democractic at the last election."

More than kicking over the traces was involved, of course, in

Brotherhood headquarters in Washington, D. C. symbol of new era.

the move to Washington. Railroad travel was no longer as crucial to union business as it had been when the headquarters were first moved to Indianapolis, then a major rail center. Sheathed in white Georgia marble, the new headquarters building overlooks the park at the foot of the United States Capitol. Its location is an apt, if perhaps unintended tribute to the growing importance of government in trade union affairs. It is this that best explains the anxiety felt by the self-reliant, craft-proud trade unionists who moved into their new quarters in 1961. For government intervention had been increasingly hostile in the late 1950s and early 1960s.

What Hutcheson termed "a rising gale of anti-unionism" manifested itself in not only so-called state right-to-work laws enacted in 18 states by 1958, but in the trend of decisions by the National Labor Relations Board, the uses made of the Taft-Hartley Law, and in the tone and slant of Congressional investigations, notably those conducted from 1957 to 1959 under Senator John L. McClellan, chairman of the Senate Select Committee on Improper Activities in the Labor and Management Field.

Although the McClellan committee, as Philip Taft pointed out, "called attention to the existence of unconscionable abuses of power, its revelations touched relatively few labor organizations. Even those unions that were shown to have abused their obligations and trust could claim that only a few of the subordinate units were affected; and where the top officers appeared to be or were proven guilty of malfeasance, many locals could claim they were innocent of the slightest wrongdoing." As Taft noted, the revelations provided few new insights into the nature and causes of racketeering. Nearly a quarter of a century earlier, Frank Duffy had rebutted the notion that legitimate unions were, in any sense, rackets. Speaking to students at Notre Dame he added, "Now mind, I want you to understand me, that does not mean to say that there is no racketeering going on. There is—by individuals in the labor movement. The union, however, should not be blamed for the acts of the individual." Duffy acknowledged that racketeers had entered the Carpenters' union at the local level. But, he said, "we did something about it." In Chicago, where hoods proposed "taking care" of Carpenters' president Tom Flynn for $5,000 a year, Flynn showed a gun and pointed to the door. In Duffy's terse comment, "They went." When a gangster waved an A. F. of L. charter before Cleveland Carpenter Harry McLaughlin, he punched his fist through it in an effective dismissal of the mobster's claim to legitimacy. Duffy concluded, "We have put them out of the organization when the evidence justified it."*

The A. F. of L.'s efforts at cleaning house of mobsters and racketeers culminated in the early 1950s with investigations of corruption within several affiliates. After the merger, the AFL-CIO in 1957 expelled the Teamsters and two other unions for failure to live up to their obligations under the Federation's constitution. The Brotherhood delegates at that convention voted against expulsion of the Teamsters on several grounds: It was an unwarranted interference with the autonomy of an affiliate; the overwhelming majority of honest Teamsters were being unfairly punished for the possible wrongdoing of a handful of officials; and the expulsion would weaken the labor movement and play into the hands of its adversaries. When the vote was announced, Teamsters secretary-treasurer John English burst out, "If Bill Hutcheson were here, you would not be doing this."

The Brotherhood's vote, apparently, aroused the curiosity, if not the ire, of the McClellan Committee. In the event, before long, numerous Committee investigators were poking and prying into the Brotherhood's affairs. Despite months of auditing and unrestricted investigation, the Committee probers were unable to uncover any improper practice in connection with the Brotherhood or in the activities of its general officers. Though it "charged" an executive board member with a possible conflict of interest and "found" that the Brotherhood "overpaid" for the writing and

---

* Unionists, however, could not always rid themselves of racketeers so readily. Dock builder Robert P. Brindell controlled the New York City building trades for half a decade when he was indicted for extortion in 1921. He was found guilty and sentenced to five to ten years in prison. Altogether 529 individuals were indicted for extortion in and around the building and construction industry of New York City at the time; of these, eighty-one were union officials, the rest were employers or public officials. Without law enforcement it is doubtful that unionists could have rid themselves of the corrupted officials.

publishing of a biography of President William L. Hutcheson, there were no prosecutions stemming from these allegations. However, the charges were magnified in the press as if the Brotherhood was a nest of racketeers.

Meanwhile, the Brotherhood had undertaken an ever-widening range of activities. In 1955, for example, the union saved Mettler's Woods, a 65-acre forest primeval in New Jersey from the woodsman's axe and picnickers' litter. It also purchased some seventy additional acres to create a natural resource where scientists could investigate the methods and processes utilized by nature in developing and maintaining a forest free from human interference. Dedicated to the memory of the late president of the Brotherhood, the William L. Hutcheson Memorial Forest was given to Rutgers University as a living laboratory.

Carpenters, along with the rest of the United States, entered the space age when Explorer I spun into orbit in 1958. Brotherhood members were on the teams that built and maintained the 5,000 miles of tracking and check centers that stretched out from Cape Canaveral. They worked on the nation's network of missile sites. Thousands of carpenters were needed to build nuclear power plants. Carpenters prepared the forms for penstocks, turbine pits and draft tubes that enabled man to realize the two-hundred-year-old dream of harnessing the great power of the Niagara River. Union men opened the St. Lawrence seaway working under a four-trade pact negotiated by the Brotherhood, the Laborers, Teamsters and Marine Engineers. Pile Drivers, Bridge, Wharf and Dock Builders Local 2375 of Wilmington, California, signed up its first woman member, Mrs. Jere Lee Cross, a deep-sea diver who set a woman's depth record of 154 feet in 1950. Ten brown-robed Trappist monks, each a skilled cabinetmaker, joined Millmen's Local 1120 in Lafayette, Oregon. And President Hutcheson remarked that the carpenter of the future would need, in addition to his union card, a helicopter pilot's license or a computer technician's certificate of training. Helicopters were already being used to put into place arched roof members as technology made inroads into the building and construction industries.

"Technological progress cannot be stopped," Hutcheson

warned. "Indeed it should not be. But the task of organized labor in the years ahead will be to win for the workers of the Nation a richer, better, and fuller life that technological progress will make possible. These things will not come automatically. They will have to be fought for and sacrificed for by strong and militant unions made up of loyal and dedicated members."

The Brotherhood also intensified its activities on behalf of the united labor movement. In 1958, for example, carpenters spear-headed successful drives against right-to-work proposals in Ohio, California, Colorado, Washington and Idaho. President M. A. Hutcheson was appointed chairman of the AFL-CIO's Committee on Social Security. In that post, he guided AFL-CIO efforts on behalf of extended, expanded and improved social security measures. The Brotherhood also sponsored the first safety institute conducted under the aegis of the Federation.

After the United States added a forty-ninth and fiftieth state (Alaska and Hawaii) and Canada, a tenth province (Newfoundland), the Brotherhood reorganized in 1960 seven unwieldy districts into ten more compact and efficient ones. By an overwhelming vote, the members voted to salvage the Brotherhood's pension program, which had a half-million dollar deficit in 1959, by increasing the per-capita charge by 25 cents a month. Deft lobbying by General Treasurer Peter E. Terzick saved the Brotherhood's Lakeland Home for retired carpenters from possible bankruptcy and the auctioneer's hammer. The Internal Revenue Service had declared that the profits derived from the Home's citrus groves were "unrelated" to the primary functions of the Brotherhood and slapped a $1.6-million tax due bill on the union. While the "profits" from citrus sales did not cover the costs of operating the home, which provided care for some 300 old-timers, the money certainly was useful. Congress, prodded by the Brotherhood, enacted a bill exempting labor unions from income taxes on such revenues.

To meet the exigencies of modern trade unionism, the members passed a referendum that empowered the Convention to conduct all business of the Brotherhood, including the election of officers. (In the past, officers had been nominated in convention and elected by referendum.) In 1960, a special convention amended the constitution to conform with new regulations imposed by the Labor-Management Reporting and Disclosure Act of 1959. Presidential candidates, Vice President Richard M. Nixon and Senator John F. Kennedy addressed the convention—a first for the Brotherhood—and were warmly received. Regional organizing offices were established to more effectively carry on drives to organize the unorganized.

The Brotherhood's Western Council of Lumber & Sawmill Workers, comprised of some 200 local unions and 13 district councils serving over 40,000 members, launched a task force to create demand for wood usage in construction. Newly designed schools featuring wood construction were urged by the Western Council and shortly became a feature of the country's expanding school construction program of the 1960s. At Seattle's World Fair, wood enhanced the futuristic buildings that dotted the fairgrounds. Foreign trade, a matter of grave concern today for trade unionists, was highlighted by the Lumber & Sawmill workers' 1950s drive against the export of logs. Ten years later, in 1968, Senator Wayne Morse succeeded, with Carpenter help, in breaking the log-export jam with a sensible limit on total exports. Carpenters also pointed out that the use of the union label on wood products was a means of defeating cheaply produced imports.

The Brotherhood was keeping a closer eye on Congress—and the Federal government—than ever before in its history. When the American Federation of Labor endorsed Adlai Stevenson against Dwight D. Eisenhower in 1952, the Brotherhood's Executive Board demurred. "The traditional non-partisan policy of the Federation must be preserved," the Board declared as the Presidential race got underway. In urging Americans after the election to rally behind President Eisenhower, Brotherhood President Hutcheson warned that "the labor movement must never allow itself to be jockeyed into a position where it is hanging on the coattails of any party." No one party, Hutcheson said, "has a monopoly on either all the virtue or all the vice that exists in political life. There are good men and bad in both parties, a fact which points up the wisdom of the policy McGuire and Gompers adopted when they made 'elect your friends and defeat your enemies' their motto."

However, as the political developments of the late 1950s and 1960s unfolded, the Brotherhood found it increasingly difficut to avoid becoming partisan, though it stuck to its determination not to hang on to any political coattails. In 1960, the delegates to the annual convention of the Ontario Council of Carpenters, representing 40,000 members, voted unanimously to back the action of the Canadian Labor Congress in founding a new political party, the liberal New Democratic Party of Canada. The delegates also urged an amendment to the Brotherhood constitution to allow Canadian carpenters to participate through their local unions in the new party. The question was thoroughly debated at the Brotherhood's 1960 convention with the majority reaffirming the Brotherhood's long-standing tradition that party politics must not enter into local union practices and meetings, although members, as are all citizens, are free to participate in the parties of their choice.

When John F. Kennedy was assassinated in Dallas on November 22, 1963, Brotherhood President Hutcheson expressed the profound sorrow and shock felt by his countrymen. The Carpenters, Hutcheson noted, had watched the development of John F. Kennedy with close attention and steadily increasing admiration from the time when he first arrived in Washington as a Congressman from Massachusetts, then as a U.S. Senator and, finally, as the President of the United States.

President Kennedy, Hutcheson declared, "was understanding, eloquent and effective in his support of the aspirations of American men and women who must work in order to live and of the millions of disadvantaged and voiceless people around the world. He had a realistic grasp of the threats to survival that this nation and the West face in dealing with Communist Russia and other power-crazed dictatorships." In assuring the support of the Brotherhood to President Lyndon B. Johnson in the trials he faced as he took over the reins of government, Hutcheson expressed the Brotherhood's confidence in President Johnson's ability and determination "not only to carry on but to carry forward our late President's program. . . . American workers look to you to start the machinery of Congress moving again so that it can complete its big backlog of unfinished business for strengthening the national economy and security."

When the Republican Party nominated Senator Barry Goldwater to run against President Johnson, Hutcheson joined James Suffridge, president of the Retail Clerks, and Lee Minton, President of the Glass Bottle Blowers (both registered Republicans), in announcing, "This is where *another* Republican gets off." Candidate Goldwater, Hutcheson pointed out, favored placing unions under anti-trust laws, limitations on industry-wide bargaining, and a national "right-to-work law." He was also against an increase in the federal minimum wage as well as a broadening of the number of workers covered.

In short, Hutcheson said, "Senator Goldwater seems to be against everything that would help the American working man. . . . His record shows that he is in complete *discord* with the policies of the Democratic Party, the Republican Party (not to include the radical right segment) and the American Labor movement."

The AFL-CIO executive council endorsement of President Johnson was unanimous.

"Whether we like it or not," *The Carpenter* stated in July, 1966, "Congress more and more makes decisions which affect our ability to improve our wages and working conditions."

A growing awareness of that proposition lay behind the Brotherhood's evolving political posture. In 1964, the union's general officers, board members and representatives voluntarily contributed two percent of their earnings to start a fund for political action and legislative work in Washington. Two years later, the Brotherhood formed the Carpenters Legislative Improvement Committee (CLIC) to solicit voluntary contributions of at least $1 from individual members.

Everyone knew about the big issues—Repeal of 14b, Situs picketing and securing prevailing wage provisions in highway bills or lease back construction where the use of private funds precluded enforcement of the Davis-Bacon Act. And there were the glamorous issues of Lyndon Johnson's Great Society backed by labor—the war on poverty measures, civil rights legislation, health and welfare measures. The Brotherhood, too, was in the forefront in achieving passage of the Federal Construction Safety Act of 1969 and of the Occupational Safety and Health Act in 1971. CLIC, however, was also caught up in nitty-gritty lobbying on behalf of minor bills which had a vital bearing on the lives of Brotherhood members. In 1966, for example, Congress passed a "boxcar bill" to stimulate construction of railroad boxcars. The shortage of such rolling stock caused layoffs among Carpenters in the West Coast lumber industry. A small town in Oregon was stymied when a government agency withheld matching funds because the local hospital was built of wood and, therefore, deemed not safe. CLIC representatives immediately went to work on Congressmen and Senators to reverse the ruling. As *The Carpenter* remarked, the work of CLIC was a bread and butter matter.

Just before the 1968 general elections, all members of the Brotherhood received an unprecedented open letter. It announced the General Executive Board's unanimous endorsement of Hubert H. Humphrey for President of the United States. While the letter reiterated the Brotherhood's long-standing policy of never telling any member how to vote, it did spell out the argument for support of Humphrey. "Since 1961," the letter stated, "a Democrat has occupied the White House and a Democratic majority has controlled Congress. During these eight years, there has not been a single recession or depression. This is the longest period of unbroken prosperity in the history of the United States. As a member of the United Brotherhood, you have made more gains in this period than in any comparable period in our history. This did not happen by accident. A favorable political climate in Washington, D. C. was necessary for this progress. This is no time to jeopardize our gains by turning over control to Mr. Nixon or Mr. Wallace, neither of whom has shown any real concern for the cause of organized labor."

The Brotherhood had backed United States efforts at halting the expansion of Communist totalitarianism in Southeast Asia. The tragic consequences of America's failure became apparent after the fall of South Vietnam as the boat people fled tyranny and the Pol

Pot regime murdered millions of hapless Cambodians. In 1968, however, Americans were confused by a war we seemingly could not win. Totalitarian leftists agitated our students while the sons of working men and women fought in Vietnam. Organized labor provided the bulk of support for the Johnson-Humphrey domestic and international policies. At the polls, that support almost carried the day. Humphrey lost by the margin of disaffection among middle-class liberals gulled by the Communists seeking victory in Vietnam.

The prosperity of the Kennedy/Johnson era helped forward what labor journalist John Herling described as a "bloodless and unadvertised revolution in the labor-management relations of the American building industry." In writing about "a jurisdictional peace treaty" negotiated by the Brotherhood and the Iron Workers to ensure the orderly installation of conveyors throughout American industry while safeguarding the job rights of the members of each union, Herling noted the revolution's roots in the 1950s when construction unions and contractors set up the National Joint Board for the Settlement of Jurisdictional Disputes. While the Board was a step in the right direction, it was not working as well as originally hoped. Unions began to clarify as best they could jurisdiction lines through voluntary agreements—"peace treaties"—such as those negotiated by the Brotherhood with the Machinists, Laborers, the Electricians as well as the Iron Workers.

At this point, as Herling commented, "we . . . see the outlines of what may become a new moral-economic dispensation. . . . In the interests of industrial peace, what is happening is the acceptance by local union leaders of the higher, responsible authority—the gradual building up of acceptance of understanding that there are larger considerations and standards universally applicable to other business agents as well as to himself."

The jurisdictional peace pacts, of course, could not eliminate disagreements altogether. Moreover, they could not freeze forever relationships constantly altered by new technology, new job assignments, even new kinds of jobs and job sites, not to mention new problems arising under new labor legislation. What was needed was a continuing forum where labor and management could periodically discuss the state of the industry and its problems. In 1959, a labor committee headed by Brotherhood president Maurice Hutcheson established with industry spokesmen the Construction Industry Joint Conference. Chaired by John T. Dunlop, the Conference met regularly to discuss broad problems and to reach constructive and equitable solutions.

As it turned out, the Conference was a stepping stone towards revamping the settlement of jurisdictional disputes. The old machinery creaked. It was plagued by costly delays. After a year of negotiations, building tradesmen and contractors signed a new pact during ceremonies at the White House as President Johnson beamed.* The President was merely a pleased host, for as he pointedly noted, "Your agreement is not the result of any govern-

---

* For labor, the new Joint Board plan was signed by President C. J. Haggerty and Secretary-Treasurer Frank Bonadio of the Building and Construction Trades Department of the AFL-CIO-CLC, representing the 3,500,000 members of its 18 affiliated international unions. For management, the plan was signed by representatives of the Associated General Contractors of America and the participating specialty contractors employers associations.

The changes in the new agreement highlight the improvements made over the old plan:

1. Establishment of a new Appeals Board, headed by an impartial umpire, to render final decisions. In the past any appeal from a decision of the National Joint Board could be taken only to the same tribunal.

2. Protection of the interests of the consumer in the settlement of jurisdictional disputes, with due regard given to such factors as efficiency and economy of operation.

3. Definition of the criteria to be used by the Joint Board in making decisions. These include decisions and agreements of record as set forth in the "Green Book"—the jurisdictional "bible" of valid agreements between affected international unions attested by the chairman of the Joint Board, established trade practice and prevailing practice in the locality.

4. Consultation with appropriate management groups in the negotiation of jurisdictional agreements between international unions.

Arrangements were made for rotating membership on the Joint Board, so that all unions and participating employers had the opportunity from year to year to serve in the decision-making process. No union representative or employer is permitted to sit in judgment on a case in which his union or company is directly involved.

ment edict or intervention. It is the successful product of long and hard negotiations and it provides a better way of settling disputes in the construction industry privately and without work stoppages."

The key to industrial peace within the building and construction industries has always been a willingness to be imaginative about jurisdiction. In 1966, for example, the Brotherhood and the Iron Workers worked out an agreement with Kaiser Steel Corporation that permits members of the two unions interchangeably to work on construction of oil drilling platforms off the West Coast. Allowing for composite crews resolves in advance work jurisdiction questions and avoids work stoppages. Cooperation also led to the first tri-trades union label when the Carpenters, the Plumbers and Electrical Workers negotiated a pre-fabricated housing agreement with Prestige Structures of Charlotte, Michigan. The three crafts shared the unionization of the manufacturer's plant; the tri-trades label guaranteed the acceptance of the union-made pre-fab houses by union carpenters, plumbers and electricians at installation sites.

A like willingness to innovate characterized the development of the Brotherhood's apprenticeship program. Training for the craft had been a knotty problem for the Brotherhood. As the 1914 convention committee on apprenticeship acknowledged, "a general plan cannot apply throughout our United Brotherhood . . . owing to the ever-varying conditions in the many localities. . . ." Nonetheless, over the years the Brotherhood sought to establish minimum standards, setting up in 1946 a standing committee on apprenticeships and developing a standard training manual that became widely used throughout the United States and Canada. The Brotherhood also cooperated from the first with the Bureau of Apprenticeship Training set up within the Department of Labor in 1937.

Though the machinery for training existed, by 1959 apprenticeship enrollments had declined. "When sufficient skilled workers are not available," First General Vice President John R. Stevenson warned, "employers tend to break down trades into simple components that can be taught quickly. This downgrades the whole stature of the trade and produces an army of half-trained workers who are capable of doing only one thing." The half-trained, Stevenson added, cannot adapt to a fast-changing technology. "Our industry has never stood still," he noted. "In my own time I saw the transition from the handsaw to the power saw take place. This was as radical a change as any we are facing today. But the men who had the proper training made the transition without too much difficulty."

To ensure that future carpenters got the proper training, the Brotherhood established in 1966 its Apprenticeship and Training Department. That the union had successfully trained 30,000 to 40,000 young men each year since 1945 was recognized by the federal government when in 1966 it granted the Brotherhood a Manpower Development Training Act contract for the development of training for disadvantaged and minority youth. Within four years, the union was operating 26 Job Corps centers scattered throughout the country, training unemployed and disadvantaged youths. To improve training, the Brotherhood brought together some thousand instructors for the first "post-graduate" in-service seminars in the industry. Carpentry Training Conferences were subsequently held in conjunction with the union's international carpenters apprenticeship contests. The first contest was held in Kansas City, Missouri, over August 15 and 16, where 54 top carpenter, mill-cabinet, and millwright apprentices vied for prizes of $1,500, $1,000 and $500 in each of the skills. It has since become a highly successful annual event.

The last decade has been an innovative one for apprenticeship training. To assist servicemen after discharge, the Brotherhood developed Project Transition. The union also developed a task analysis of all craft areas, pioneering in the use of photographic detailing of work processes. The Performance Evaluated Training System (PETS) evolved out of the Brotherhood experience in the field, which has meant more flexibility in apprenticeships. For example, in 1974, the upper age limit for apprentices was removed and pre-apprenticeship experience was taken into account.

Apprenticeships were among the targets of the civil rights movement of the 1960s. Though the Brotherhood organized black and white carpenters from its first days, there is no question but that some discrimination did exist within the building and construction industry. In the unions it was the exception, not the rule, and certainly not typical of the Brotherhood. Nonetheless, there were some who went after labor as a scapegoat and sought to break up unionism. Bayard Rustin, the organizer of the 1964 March on Washington, however, warned against the lowering of standards, particularly in the apprenticeship system. Along with his mentor, A. Philip Randolph, Rustin believed that the labor movement was the best instrument for the advancement of Negro hopes and aspirations. Black workers, Rustin repeatedly declared, wanted to be equally trained and equally skillful with their co-workers. "They certainly did not want to be declared 'second class workers' any more than they wanted to be 'second class citizens.' "

The founders of the union wrote into its constitution a principle which still stands: "We recognize that the interests of all classes of labor are identical regardless of occupation, nationality, religion or color, for a wrong done to one is a wrong done to all." Carpenters were among the first, if not the only union to elect a black international officer in the 1880s. It hired black organizers to organize black and white workers in the South, though it had to give way to local "customs" to the extent of forming separate black and white local unions. (Remember, there were those who would not organize black workers at all, north or south.) Local unions in the North were integrated. So, naturally, at the height of the 1960s civil rights agitation, the Brotherhood had no trouble in reasserting its tradition. It took the initiative and directed racially separated local unions to merge before obligated to do so by law.* Incidently, opposition to the merger of such locals was strongest among the blacks.

---

* At a special board meeting, Brotherhood local unions were directed to comply with four points enumerated by the AFL-CIO-CLC Building and Construction Trades Department, adopted on June 21, 1963. These were:

"1. Local unions are to accept into membership any applicant who meets the required qualifications regardless of race, creed, color or national origin.

"2. If a local union has an agreement which provides for, and operates, an exclusive hiring hall, all applicants for employment are to be placed upon the hiring list in accordance with the applicable law and their collective bargaining agreement. There is to be no identification of applicants as to

Though the Brotherhood was not guilty of discrimination, it joined with other building and construction trades unionists in cooperating with the Recruitment and Training Program, an outreach program inspired by Randolph and Rustin. RTP's experts found, much to their own surprise, that minority youngsters were not applying for existing programs for a variety of reasons, including the fact that high school counselors seldom advised youngsters to enter a blue collar field. Moreover, though well represented in the

race, creed, color or national origin, and they are to be referred without discrimination as their turn comes up on the hiring list, if their qualifications meet those required by the employer.

"3. If the local unions do not have an exclusive hiring hall, but do have a referral system set forth in their collective bargaining agreement, qualified applicants for employment are to be referred without discrimination as to race, creed, color or national origin.

"4. With regard to the application for, or employment of apprentices, local unions shall accept, and refer, such applicants in accordance with their qualifications and there shall be no discrimination as to race, creed, color or national origin, and the local unions shall adhere strictly to their apprenticeship standards."

In addition, the General President was instructed:

"to take whatever steps may be necessary to bring about promptly the elimination of racially separated local unions, if it is found that any such local unions exist.

However, the Board also noted: "Any such unions as may exist have been kept segregated not at the behest of our Brotherhood, but because of the insistence of their own members who are members of minority groups.

"We have decided that to be consistent our Brotherhood cannot maintain segregation at the request of the same minority groups who are justifiably anxious to wipe out all segregation.

"However, with the best will in the world to be helpful in correcting any discrimination, we cannot under any circumstances permit the imposition of quotas, either by a government agency or by any outside private organization. We consider quotas totally undemocratic and out of line with sound trade union practice.

"Union membership must depend upon meeting the established qualifications, and jobs must be assigned on a first-come, first-served basis. To do otherwise would be to create new discriminations."

194

carpenters, the bricklayers and in the so-called "trowel trades," black participation was lower in the mechanical trades where higher educational requirements and other cultural factors not related to discrimination were operative. So RTP's outreach program not only recruited black youth but also offered special tutoring to enable them to compete without lowering standards in the crafts. As a consequence of RTP efforts and those of the craft unions, the overall situation improved dramatically within a few short years. Some idea of the gains is provided by comparing the statistics of 1960 and 1968. Non-whites made up 2.4 percent of the total 85,682 apprentices in the United States in 1960; by the first half of 1968, approximately 9.4 percent of the 26,156 newly enrolled apprentices came from minority groups. A Brotherhood study of pre-apprenticeship and apprenticeships in 1971 showed that minorities comprised 25.7% of new entrants over 1966–1971, and 16.9 percent of those who completed training.

Though the Brotherhood increasingly found itself contending with government, its major gains were scored in collective bargaining, and not without struggle. It took a 20-month strike over 1955–1956 to win union conditions at Fir-Tex, an insulating board manufacturer. Ten years later, maintenance carpenters joined some 60,000 workers in a nine-month struggle involving some 26 unions against the nation's copper barons. During the strike, which affected 11 companies in 23 states, the AFL-CIO-CLC urged trade unionists to "adopt a copper striker's family." Federation affiliates donated over $700,000 for distribution to the strikers and their families as the copper bosses sought to starve workers into submission. A breakthrough was achieved in the ninth month after 12 days of talks initiated by President Johnson. But the gravest crisis the Brotherhood faced in the decade was in the forests of Northern Canada where loggers fought bosses and Communists to win a trade-union victory.

By 1959, the Brotherhood was the second largest union in Canada with 76,501 carpenters, millworkers, millwrights, bushworkers in locals and affiliated trades groups. Yet, its foothold in the northern woods was precarious indeed. The bushworkers had a long (and spotty) history of organization. The Industrial Workers of the World had tried in vain to organize them just before World

War I. Company controlled police and goon squads smashed an independent union's effort in the 1920s. The remnants joined the Brotherhood in 1936, but progress was slow. Conditions were terrible. As J. G. Pesheau, later Secretary-Treasurer of the Northern Ontario District Council of Lumber & Sawmill Workers, described them, bushworkers shared boiled rotten salt pork and beans with rats in tar-paper shacks with no windows, or in musty sod-dugouts. A spruce pole in the bush served as a toilet. Horses were treated much better because a horse cost the company money.

A long strike won union recognition in 1946, but little else. Communists exploited worker grievances to no good effect. They also spent union money for their own political purposes. The Brotherhood, finally, had to intervene, suspending the officers and placing three locals under the trusteeship of District 7 (Canada) executive board member Andrew V. Cooper.

It was not a happy situation. As Pesheau remarked, "the suspended officers commenced forming another Independent Union, and through misrepresentation and outright lies and through the fact that they were known to the bushworker, whereas the new Organizers of the Brotherhood were not, they were able to cause turmoil and split the membership."

Cooper made the best of a bad situation. He secured a small wage increase in negotiations and a union shop with a check-off of dues. This allowed union organizers entry into the northern woods, enabled them to resolve grievances expeditiously, and opened the door for further gains. The Independent Union died, the local unions were freed of trusteeship and bushworkers were once again running their own affairs.

In ten years, 1951 to 1961 wages were almost doubled, rising, for example, from $7.15 a day to $13.84 a day for laborers (excluding bonus payments). But the most dramatic gains were in conditions: Pesheau is our witness:

> Compared to the vermin-infested hovels that were the lot of the bushworker . . . what do we have today? We have well-built, well-ventilated, central, thermostatically-controlled heat, tile or linoleum floor (scrubbed and disinfected at least once a week), cubicled bunkhouse where we live, good single spring beds with mattresses

and clean sheets, pillow cases and blankets, and yes, even nylon bedcovers. We have immaculate wash rooms with hot and cold running water, inside flush toilets and showers, laundry facilities supplied by the Company, first-aid kits galore, recreation rooms with T.V. and a free show once a week. The food, generally speaking, is served on a cafeteria basis and is the best . . . all you want of it! It would put most hotels to shame. This is served in a modern, up-to-date kitchen and dining room where equipment includes automatic coffee makers, automatic dishwashers, propane stoves and ovens, and where our members, the cookery staff, take pride in producing good food and keeping things clean.

That was the beginning. With a majority of bushworkers of Ontario organized, the Brotherhood was ready to organize the rest as well as the loggers of Newfoundland. The campaign to organize the loggers began in 1955, even though the Brotherhood had long established local craft unions in the province, when the Newfoundland Lumberman's Association proposed affiliation. With the approval of a majority of its members, the Association finally joined the Brotherhood in the summer of 1957. The International Woodworkers of America (IWA) had also organized two major loggers' locals in Newfoundland. Unable to reach an agreement on a contract, the IWA locals struck. It was a bitter affair. Newfoundland's legislature passed a law that just about banned the IWA from Newfoundland's woods. The strike was lost, the IWA decertified and its locals disbanded. After the strike failed, the desperate loggers turned to the Brotherhood. Given the extraordinary sensitivity inherent in the situation, the Brotherhood responded with caution. (During the time the IWA was disbarred from organizing in Newfoundland, the Brotherhood made no effort to re-enter the Province.) A committee met with Canadian Labor Congress (CLC) officers to seek assurance that the Brotherhood was right to resume organizing in the Newfoundland woods, given the unhappy lost IWA strike. Reassured, the Brotherhood launched a drive to organize the Newfoundland loggers. It was a success.

Meanwhile, however, the IWA lodged raiding charges against the Brotherhood with the CLC. After much palaver, the CLC executive council adopted a report which found the Brotherhood

New beginnings in apprenticeship. Blacks and women enter trade in larger number in late 1960s and 1970s.

innocent of any raiding charges but also maintained that the Brotherhood should halt all organizing activities on behalf of the Newfoundland loggers. The Brotherhood delegates to the Congress's 1962 convention walked out in protest. The General Executive Board decided to withhold the payment of per capita while remaining affiliated with the Congress until the matter was ironed out. The Newfoundland Loggers' scored their first breakthrough in an agreement with the Province's major pulp companies.

The Brotherhood soon became the major union in Newfoundland. But the task of organizing and of improving the working conditions of the woodsmen in the Canadian north woods continued. A Canadian newspaper reported that workers at non-union camps, "were expected to repair chain saws and other equipment in the cramped, rough wood bunkhouses where they slept in double-tier beds. For days there was no water for drinking or washing. There was water for the horses, but none for the men."

Kapuskasing Lumber and Sawmill Workers went on strike after months of futile negotiatons over wages and improved working conditions. The strike was complicated by continued cutting by local settlers licensed to cut timber on crown lands in Northern Ontario. Residents were required to do their own cutting but many of the "licensees" were contractors hiring others to do the cutting. This allowed for unfair conditions and took work away from union men. It was also a situation guaranteed to exacerbate feelings in the strike-bound woods.

On February 11, 1963 tragedy struck. In the chill dawn, at Reesor Landing, near Kapuskasing, Brotherhood members Leo Fortier, Irenee Fortier and A. Drouin were gunned down by a group of part-time loggers. Nine others were wounded in the firing upon the unarmed strikers. After the shooting, 237 strikers were arrested on charges of rioting; nineteen part-time loggers were arrested and charged with non-capital murder.

The shooting had an unintended consequence. The company and the union agreed to turn the contract dispute over to arbitration and end the walkout. And so trade unionism came to the Canadian north woods.

XII

THE FUTURE BELONGS TO
THE PREPARED

Brotherhood negotiators were not making any headway in bargaining with the Tigerton Lumber Company. Lawrence Swanke, the owner of the small Wisconsin firm, also owned the store and gas station where his workers shopped as well as the town electric power plant. When a reporter questioned him about the situation, he said, "You know as well as I do that a lot of these people would never be able to manage their own affairs, if the company didn't do it for them. Everyone's trying to make me look like some kind of bastard, but we are helping our employees. Most of them are much better off when they get their paychecks, and their food and light bills are already paid. You should know that. You know how some people are."

As it turned out, the "paternal" Mr. Swanke did not know his employees all that well. They went on strike, held out for three months in late 1970 until the company capitulated. They won a modest wage increase, plant-wide seniority, dues-checkoff and a shortened probationary period. More to the point, the company also agreed not to harass any employee for not shopping at the company store or service station; employee bills were not to be deducted from their paychecks without written authorization approved by the union.

Local Union 2806's disciplined response to retrogressive paternalism was in sharp contrast to the violent upheavals sweeping the college campuses as the young chafed at authority and demanded, in M. A. Hutcheson's percipient phrase, "reforms that range from the justified to the absurd."

"When liberty is threatened, when exploitation is uncovered, when National security is endangered," Hutcheson once remarked, "working people are the first to respond with everything they have. . . . Over the years they used the picket line to wipe out injustices, elevate living standards, and redress wrongs to one man or to a group. But they have little time for picket lines over the length of hair or the right to go barefooted. . . . The draft dodgers, the flag burners, the dope users, mostly come from an affluent background. They neither felt pangs of hunger nor experienced the discipline that making one's own way imposes. Consequently they are long on idealism and short on experience, which can differentiate between the possible and the impossible."

Idealism backed by experience was evident as Carpenter negotiators patiently developed improvements in pension coverage. For decades carpenters protected themselves against the vissicitudes of old age through contributions to the Brotherhood's pension fund. Then Social Security and employer-paid benefits expanded that protection. But in the fragmented building and construction industry, where workers frequently moved from job to job, employer-financed pension benefits did not "travel." Contracts, typically, provided that pension payments be made only in the district where work is performed, so a worker who worked elsewhere found his benefits reduced, if not lost altogether. New York City carpenters made the first breakthrough in 1965 when the New York District Council secured pensions "portable" throughout the greater New York Metropolitan area.

The notion of a "portable" pension proved attractive. The 1970 Brotherhood convention instructed the General Executive Board and union officers to develop a new approach that would (1) make it easier for local unions without a pension to negotiate one with their employers, and (2) provide a vehicle for increasing the portability of existing pension plans.

Meanwhile, a subcommittee of the United States Senate held

hearings on the whole pension question. Much of the testimony was shocking. Many pension programs, particularly those provided unilaterally by employers, failed to provide proper funding, so that the money was not available when employees reached retirement age. Even in some plans negotiated by unions, rigid vesting qualifications eliminated many employees. In the Brotherhood's experience, for example, it was difficult to provide pensions for members in local unions with fewer than one hundred members. The base in such locals is not broad enough to provide decent coverage at a reasonable cost.

On October 11, 1971, General President Hutcheson announced the establishment of the Carpenters Labor-Management Fund, which would operate two separate pension plans, one for industrial members and the other for construction members. Each, of course, was tailored to meet the special problems and needs of the members covered. For each sector, the respective plan facilitates bargaining for pensions, offers portability and ensures greater financial security for the funds. The Brotherhood also developed a "Pro-Rata Agreement," which provided a vehicle for portability for existing funds. As individual plans signed up, members working under one plan could work under the jurisdiction of another without losing credits for a pension if the requirements for a pro-rata plan were met. When the time came for retirement, a member would draw a proportional pension from each of the pension funds worked under.

"We look forward to the day when all our members will have continuous pension coverage no matter where they work," Hutcheson said. "All local unions and councils now have the opportunity to take action which will help to assure their members of that kind of pension coverage."

Progress often entails paradox. Organized labor's success in providing adequate pensions for working men and women, in this instance, was ultimately responsible for the closing of the Carpenters' Home in Lakeland, Florida, and for the termination of the membership pension.

New state regulations for old age care prompted a review of the operation of the Home in 1972. Operational costs already exceeded per capita tax by $20,000 a month. The new regulations would have required a half-million dollars or more in capital expenditures, requiring a substantial additional tax on the members at a time when the number of residents was steadily declining. After 42 years of successful operation, the General Executive Board reluctantly urged closing the home. The membership by a two-to-one vote in referendum agreed.

For much the same reasons—improved social security and medicare benefits, the expansion of private pension plans—members were reluctant to increase per capita to maintain the membership pension. In 1973, a referendum thumbed down an increase needed to maintain the pension at $30 a month. The growth in the number of pensioners, roughly 68,000 by 1978, cut into the funds still further, reducing benefits to $14 a month. Since the members had indicated, time and time again, that they did not wish to increase the Pension Fund per capita sufficiently to maintain the benefit at the $30 level established in 1966, the Board, in a special report to the 1978 convention, recommended its termination. In its place, it proposed a Benevolent Program, providing an increased death and disability benefit.

The closing down of the Home was one of those "tremendous changes" noted by Maurice A. Hutcheson on his retirement at age 73 on March 1, 1972:

> When I was starting out, the son or daughter of a carpenter who got to college was a rarity indeed. Today, thousands upon thousands of members' children are making fine records in universities all over the United States and Canada.
>
> At the start of my career there were no such things as negotiated pensions, Social Security, unemployment insurance, group health insurance, or any of the other protections which make for better and more secure lives for working people.
>
> In all the many struggles that took place in the legislative halls and at the bargaining table to secure these measures, the United Brotherhood played a vital role. It affords me considerable satisfaction to know that I had some small part in these achievements.
>
> However, the real heroes in the endless struggle to bring about better, happier and more secure conditions for working people are

the thousands upon thousands of dedicated Brotherhood members and hundreds upon hundreds of hardworking Local Union and Council officers.

Day by day, they have been on the firing line, and they have fought the good fight in good times and bad. The cooperation they have given me and the General Office over the years constitutes the bricks and mortar of the foundation upon which our Brotherhood rests.

After 50 years of continuous membership in the union he had served so well, it is small wonder then that Hutcheson became President Emeritus replete "with wonderful memories as well as great satisfaction."

"I know," he added, "that members who joined our organization in the past few years are not too excited about the battles that went on 40 or 50 years ago. However, the past struggles are a part of our heritage and as such they should not be totally ignored." History, too, he warned, "seemingly has a way of repeating itself." It was a sentiment that the Brotherhood's new president, William Sidell, was soon to repeat, though in somewhat different words.

Sidell's administration began auspiciously. The Brotherhood's membership reached a peak of 857,000 members in 1973. Yet best estimates indicated that the union had only about 25 to 30 percent of the residential carpenters organized. Carpenters were pinched by unemployment in 1970. In California, for example, outside of the Los Angeles area, carpenter unemployment varied between 25 and 30 percent. In Canada, despite a pressing need for one million new housing units a year in Ontario alone, construction unemployment was more than triple the general 6.5% rate of joblessness. But the pinch of the early 1970's became an ugly slash by 1976 when the AFL-CIO-CLC Building and Construction Trades Department reported joblessness among construction workers running 60% in the Northeast, 34.8 percent in the Mid-Atlantic region, 22.9 percent in the Midwest, 20.5 percent in the West and 24.5 percent in the Southern United States.

As ominous as the threats of unemployment were certain rumblings among employers. In 1972, for example, C. T. Love, president of a small Louisville general contracting firm got together with six other area contractors to form the Kentuckiana chapter of the Associated Builders and Contractors (ABC), a national association of open-shop contractors. Within a few months, the chapter, which covered all of Kentucky and Southern Indiana, had grown to 56 members with separate contracts for over $30-million worth of construction.

"ABC members," declared Dave Gale, president of the Georgia chapter, "are enlisting in an army that is going to fight a long war against an enemy that is trying to destroy free enterprise in this country. The enemy is varied, but in the frontline with those with the union label and right behind them is the Federal Government."

Over the years 1970 to 1973, more than $10-billion worth of construction, which formerly would have been considered union, had gone non-union. In 1972, 32 percent of all construction nationally went to open-shop contractors. The volume of big open-shop contractors rose from 14 percent in 1974 to 48 percent in 1975. During the same period, three non-union firms alone accounted for eight-and-a-half billion dollars in construction in the United States. Some areas of the country dropped from nearly 100 percent union commercial and industrial work in 1974 to less than 35 percent in 1975.

"Not since the 1920's," Sidell declared in response to the situation confronting the Carpenters, "have the employers been so thoroughly organized for an assault on union wages and working conditions."

Born in Chicago, Illinois, on May 30, 1915, Sidell by temperament and training was well equipped to cope with the challenges confronting the Brotherhood. In 1920 he moved to Los Angeles, California with his mother and father, a carpenter-cabinet maker. Sturdy and affable, though competitive, young Sidell played high school football and ran on the track team. After completing his formal education, he followed in his father's footsteps, becoming an apprentice in Local 721. His first elected office was as warden of the 4,500-member local union. In 1957, he was elected Secretary-Treasurer of the Los Angeles County District Council of Carpenters, the largest in the country with over 55,000 members.

Sidell liked to rise early, and most mornings arrived at his desk before 7:30 a.m. Active in California affairs, he became a vice president of the California Labor Federation, AFL-CIO. He served on the Governor's Advisory Commission on Housing Problems. In 1962, he was elected as GEB member for the 8th District. When the late Finlay C. Allan moved up to fill a vacancy in 1964, Sidell was appointed Second General Vice President. Following Allan's death, he became First General Vice President in April 1970, taking on the responsibilities for apprenticeship and training, fields in which he had a deep interest.

Sidell served on the Construction Industry Stabilization Committee where he learned something of the importance of government to the economy as well as something of the importance of autonomy to the labor movement. On February 23, 1971, President Richard M. Nixon temporarily suspended the Davis-Bacon Act, citing "excessive wage and price increases" as an explanation of his action. AFL-CIO President Meany termed the suspension "an open invitation to unscrupulous employers to exploit workers by competitive undermining of fair wages and labor standards." The action, Meany added, "attempts to correct . . . mass unemployment in a period of inflation brought about by the unwise monetary and fiscal policies of the President and his economic advisors, by penalizing a single segment of the working population." President Nixon revoked the suspension but, then, invoking powers granted him by the Wage Stabilization Act of 1970, he issued an Executive Order creating a Construction Industry Stabilization Committee.

Each craft in the building and construction trades was required to have a board of its own to examine contracts negotiated after March 29, 1970, to see whether or not the wage increases obtained conformed to a formula embodied in the President's Executive Order. Roughly, that formula provided that wage patterns over 1961–1969 were not to be exceeded. The final authority for determining the appropriateness of any negotiated wage increases rested with the tri-partite Stabilization Committee, chaired by John T. Dunlop.

President Nixon subsequently established, in October, 1971, an overall Pay Board with labor and industry representation. However, as the AFL-CIO-CLC Executive Council pointed out, the Pay Board turned out "not to be tripartite. It is not independent and autonomous. The Pay Board represents Government control. It represents political and business interests." AFL-CIO President Meany and the labor members of the Pay Board resigned in protest, refusing to be "a part of the window dressing for this system of unfair and inequitable Government control of wages for the benefit of business profits."

However, in sharp contrast to the difficulties encountered by the Pay Board, the Construction Industry Stabilization Committee succeeded in achieving flexible and equitable procedures for stabilizing wages in construction. It did so because it was truly an autonomous tripartite board, which facilitated the settlement of labor disputes in the industry with due regard for the interests of the workers and the maintenance of free collective bargaining. While carpenters felt that they fell short of keeping pace with increases in the cost of living, nonetheless, the Brotherhood secured through bargaining (approved by the CISC) an average wage rate, including fringe benefits, of $9.39 an hour at the end of 1973, roughly an increase of $1.75 an hour over 1971.

The lesson was not lost on the Carpenters. While the union successfully opposed the renewal of the Wage Stabilization Act in 1974, it maintained the mechanism created by the President in the jointly-financed Craft Board. This voluntary Board's work, providing assistance to collective bargaining, has been reinforced by the growth of international agreements between the Brotherhood and major contractors and trade associations. In 1974, there were 1272 such agreements; in 1978, there were 2127. These agreements, as Sidell has pointed out, "provide protection of our trade autonomy and increased employment opportunities for our membership."

The Brotherhood also joined other unions in coordinated bargaining with such industrial giants as General Electric and Westinghouse and in the nonferrous metals industry. Carpenters, Laborers and Iron Workers negotiated composite crew agreements in chimney, stack, silo and cooling tower construction, including slip-form construction, a revolutionary building technique in the erection of super-tall and hyperbolic water-cooling towers. To generate jobs and speed nuclear power plant construction without stoppages, the Brotherhood joined the AFL-CIO-CLC Building and Construction Trades Department in negotiating a national agreement with the four companies which have built more than 80 percent of the operating nuclear power plants in the United States— Bechtel Power Corporation, Ebasco Services, Stone & Webster Engineering, and United Engineers & Constructors, Inc.

Though Brotherhood affiliates enjoy a long-standing tradition of autonomy in collective bargaining matters, the General Office took the initiative in developing uniform wage and working conditions for members employed in industrial maintenance. Local collective bargaining mechanisms had failed to deal with the unique needs of that industry. In this highly competitive field, contractors, typically, bid for maintenance work at such industrial installations as steel mills, oil refineries, and other industrial complexes throughout the country. To develop and strenghten union standards, the Brotherhood, in 1955, helped establish with the Building Trades unions the General Presidents' Project Maintenance Agreement and, later, it took the leadership in establishing similar agreements with the National Erectors Association, with Westinghouse (for turbine overhauls), a tri-trades Power Generation Agreement and similar pacts with other associations. In 1973, there were some 240 contractors involved in various industrial maintenance agreements, and the program worked so well that, by 1978, more than 660 contractors had signed on. The gain in industrial maintenance work for Brotherhood members throughout North America demonstrates the value of such agreements. In the four years following the 1974 recession there were almost 14-million manhours of work for Brotherhood members under the General Presidents' Project Maintenance Agreement and almost 13-million manhours of work under the National Maintenance Agreement.

The cost of jurisdictional squabbling was graphically illustrated when the courts upheld a million-dollar judgment against the Brotherhood in the Noranda Aluminum case. In the erection of a $100,000,000 aluminum plant in Missouri, a contractor awarded the work in question to the millwrights in writing at a pre-job conference, but later refused to stand behind the award and refused to remove members of another trade who moved in on the work.

The millwrights stopped work over their primary dispute with the contractor. The court, however, disregarded the contractor's award as well as the Brotherhood's efforts to resolve the matter. The law as it now stands prohibits, in effect, a strike to compel employers to re-assign work once underway. The judgment is the largest ever paid by the Brotherhood. In another case, the union paid $350,000. Fortunately, those cases are the only two of such magnitude.

Jurisdictional squabbles, Sidell remarked in 1974, "create many serious problems for the healthy growth of unionization in the construction industry. It is no accident that $30 billion or $35 billion worth of construction has gone to non-union contractors in recent years. . . . We stand ready to explore any avenues which hold promise of creating an orderly vehicle for resolving jurisdictional differences between trades."

Among these avenues have been voluntary agreements between the unions directly involved, such as the master agreement defining millwright and ironworker rigging jurisdictions. After years of conflict over logging operations, plywood plants, sawmills and other forest-plant industries in the United States and Canada, the Brotherhood and the International Woodworkers of America formally decided to work together, particularly in organizing new operations and in coordinated bargaining at already organized plants. The Brotherhood also agreed to a no-raiding pact with the Teamsters. A new type of industrial pre-heater necessitated a new accord between millwrights and boilermakers. A new generation of turbines, nuclear power plants, Bailey meters and power-actuated cylinders required an agreement on work assignments for millwrights, plumbers and pipefitters. And in 1979, the Wood, Wire and Metal Lathers International Union concluded nearly 80 years of existence by affiliation with the Brotherhood, bringing to a happy conclusion some long-standing jurisdictional squabbles.

One consequence of such voluntary agreements has been a decided improvement in the relations with the AFL-CIO-CLC Building Trades Department. Increasingly, the Brotherhood has cooperated with the Department on common legislative and political goals. Carpenters participated in the "summit" negotiating committee that worked out with the National Constructors Association a precedent-setting agreement for uniform national work rules and a system of financial penalties in the area of jurisdictional disputes. For the first time, a contractor who makes an unreasonable mis-assignment can be assessed up to $10,000 for the first violation and even higher penalties for subsequent ones. Fines can be levied against an international union that fails to take "prompt and appropriate" action against a local that strikes or pickets a job to further a jurisdictional dispute. Penalties range from $2,500 for a small union to $10,000 for a large one. An impartial umpire decides if rules are violated, and he fixes the penalty. Separate trusts were set up to receive the fines. The Employer Trust finances research and study in the area of manpower use and recruitment. The Building Trades Trust finances research on the origin and prevention of labor disputes.

"If we are to build a better America," Sidell declared at the Brotherhood's 1974 convention, "we must build more and better housing." Our residential building system, he argued, is crumbling drastically. "This is dramatically illustrated not only by reduced housing starts, but also by the most recent rise in interest rates to 9 percent or more in available mortgage monies." (Since then, inflation has pushed mortgage interest rates into double digits.) High interest rates and inflation, Sidell said, place housing out of the reach of the poor and many middle-class Americans. To stabilize the housing market as well as to stimulate construction of needed housing, Sidell urged that "the time has come to remove the housing industry from the free enterprise banking system. In its place, I propose that the Federal Government broaden the Federal Housing Administration and provide funds directly to the citizens at interest rates commensurate with the need of that industry. Not the nine, ten and eleven percent where we are headed today, but more in the four or five percent category."

Sidell's proposal stirred up a good deal of controversy. It also drew attention to what he termed "the seed pod of the non-union segment of the construction industry." The Carpenters' concern for better housing, he declared, also carried with it an obligation. "We must bring to these thousands of non-union workers the integrity, respectability and security that our United Brotherhood has to offer." Sidell reminded the delegates of the great changes the union had undergone over the years: "We are a craft union and we are an industrial union." The key to the union's future, he said, is organization. "When we organize a non-union homebuilder we eliminate the training ground of the non-union craftsmen and eliminate an unfair competitor within our industry. When we organize a shop, plant or factory, we eliminate that threat to the well-being of our membership and the fair union shop."

That year, the Brotherhood launched two drives against the open shop—the Coordinated Housing Organization Program (CHOP) and the Voluntary Organizing Committee (VOC). Residential building had been the traditional backbone of the Brotherhood. Journeymen, typically, learned their craft building homes and apartment houses. World War II marked a drift away from residential construction to defense and industrial construction that continued in the post-war period. The revival of home demand after the war sparked a new development, on-site production housing with its myriad of specialty subcontractors. Many of these started as small non-union homebuilders, who, as they gained in size, remained notoriously anti-union. The Brotherhood, for its part, missed the opportunity for organizing a growing segment of construction. Perhaps organizing industrial plants was, in a way, easier; perhaps journeymen were fully occupied in industrial and urban construction. For whatever reason, the Brotherhood lost its predominant position in the housing industry. By the 1970s, only 25 to 30 percent of the housing built in the United States was built by union labor.

CHOP was the Brotherhood's answer to the crisis, to jerrybuilt non-union housing. It was aimed at the half-million carpentry workers engaged in home construction who were not members of the Brotherhood. CHOP, declared *The Carpenter*, "is a program for every state and provincial council, every construction district council, and every construction local union in our Brotherhood! It is not voluntary. . . . It is *mandatory*, a *must*, a *duty*, an *obligation*, a *necessity for survival!*"

The Volunteer Organizing Committee (VOC) program was conveived by the union as a continent-wide "second front," with teams of volunteer organizers in every one of the Brotherhood's 2,500 local unions in the United States and Canada. The goal, as phrased by President Sidell, was to reach "the million or more workers in industrial plants throughout North America who might be . . . *and should be* . . . members of the United Brotherhood." Organizing guidebooks, sample leaflets, and one-minute radio "spot" commercials were among the aids prepared by the organizing department. Regional seminars briefed local and district leaders. Special conferences, such as those held for the underwater divers, millwrights and floor coverers, emphasized organizing within the context of the particular problems faced by each group. The Brotherhood also participated in the building trades "pilot" organizing campaign in Los Angeles, which recruited 10,000 new members within one month (January of 1979).

Unfortunately, just as CHOP and VOC got underway, the country experienced extraordinary inflation and high unemployment, circumstances not conducive to successful organization. Unemployment in construction hit as high as 90 pecent in some areas with 30 to 40 percent typical in far too many others. Over the four years ending December 31, 1977, the Brotherhood lost 68,687 members; 59,868 were construction members, 8,710 were industrial members. Without CHOP and VOC, it would, no doubt, have suffered a far greater loss. Despite stiffened opposition, the Brotherhood won 48 percent of the 384 representation elections conducted by the National Labor Relations Board over 1973–1977 as compared to the all-union average of 46 percent. Moreover, it secured 274 voluntary recognition agreements over the same four-year period.

William Konyha, who succeeded Sidell as President of the Brotherhood in 1980, once noted, "The enemies of organized labor are smarter today than they were a hundred years ago. And they now have at their command a whole new arsenal of anti-union weapons."

Cleverly exploiting legitimate concerns, the National Right To Work Legal Defense Foundation devised an advertising campaign centered on alleged violations of individual rights and civil liberties to help create an anti-union climate. On popular television shows, union leaders are almost invariably portrayed as goons or racketeers.

While Madison Avenue techniques erode public confidence in trade unionism, highly-paid consultants devise ways, not only to get around the law but to exploit its loopholes in order to weaken trade unions. In Ohio, for example, Brotherhood organizers ran up against a consulting firm that offered seminars to management that taught employers how to delay bargaining and how to induce their employees to file union decertification petitions.

Some of the new union-busting techniques are old ones, brushed up and brought up to date. When Ethel Johnson decided to help the Brotherhood organize Sav-A-Stop, a wholesale distributor of health and beauty products at Orange Park, Florida, she was called into the manager's office. "When I got there," she said, "he wanted me to write five sentences that he was going to dictate. Then he had me write the alphabet in capital letters and then in small letters. Then he told me to sign it. . . . Then he told me to sit in this tiny room, like a closet and they kept me there for over two hours. Someone would open the door just wide enough to peek in but wouldn't let me out. Finally they told me that someone kidnapped the Burton kids and they knew I did it so they said they were taking me for a lie detector test."

Ethel Johnson was then taken to the next county and threatened with the loss of her job and arrest by the police. She was subjected to a polygraph test. Then the management brought Ms. Johnson back to the plant and told her they wanted to take her for another lie-detector test at a later time. She refused to go so they said they had no other choice but to "terminate" her. "They wouldn't let me go and get my sweater or my car keys or anything. They made me wait while someone went back to my locker and got my things."

Old-time finks surely would have enjoyed this bit of advice encapsulated in an Associated Builders' and Contractors' bulletin:

> There are a number of tradesmen who, because of their distaste for the policies of the union to which they belong (perhaps they are unwilling to belong and do so as a requirement of keeping a job), would be willing to attend union meetings and give a report of the subject matter of the meeting, or by means of a pocket recorder, record it, or better yet, by means of a small concealed short range

radio transmitter and remote (off site) receiver and recorder, record the entire meeting.

Activity of this type comes under the category of "an ounce of prevention" and we feel every effort should be made to develop these information gathering means. The value per dollar spent, should far exceed that of any activity designed to counter an organized assault.

Harassment and delay, however, remain among the most effective weapons in the anti-labor arsenal. As Pauline Frazier, a knurling-machine operator at Craftool in Fort Worth, Texas, testified, in 1977, before the House Subcommittee on Labor Relations, her employer delayed negotiations with the Brotherhood by scheduling meetings a month apart, claiming each time that he had to be out of town. Two members of the bargaining committee were "promoted" to supervisory positions they could ill afford to turn down because of family obligations. Subsequently, they were both fired. Other workers were called in by foremen and told to sign decertification statements. One could describe them as modern versions of the "yellow dog contract." One woman was so torn by her fear of the employer (she signed) and her desire for a union that she had a mental breakdown. When the decertifications were dismissed by the NLRB as false and forced, the employer simply ignored the board decision. "We've been cheated," declared Pauline Frazier. "We're out on a limb, and the employer is sawing it off."

When Roger Taft, a sawmill worker in Glide, Oregon, joined a union drive at the Little River Lumber Company, he thought he would be protected by the law. Did not the law "guarantee" workers' rights to organize, to bargain collectively and to choose freely their own representatives? He served as the Brotherhood's organizing committee chairman, passed out authorization cards; 38 out of 43 of his fellow workers signed up. Enraged, the owner carried out his threat to sell if the plant went union and everyone was fired. After a few days, everyone was rehired, except Taft and two other union activists. The union filed unfair labor practice complaints with the NLRB. The company offered the three union men six weeks back pay *if* they would drop the complaint and sign a statement that they would never seek employment with the company.

"What was I to do?" Taft asked. With a wife and small child, a newly-built house, mounting bills, Taft believed he had little choice but to sign, especially since all that the attorneys could promise was a court battle of up to four years. "Something must be done to stop the lengthy, drawn-out lawsuits," Taft told the House Subcommittee. "Workers like myself simply can't afford to fight against companies. To guys like me, long litigation is really intimidation."

Reverend Harry J. Bowie, an Episcopal minister, was drawn into Brotherhood efforts to organize Croft Metals of McComb, Mississippi, by his concern for the welfare of his parishioners. Like Roger Taft, he believed that the law could protect their rights. And so it seemed to do when the NLRB ordered the company to engage in "good-faith" bargaining. After months of obstruction, however, the company finally balked, simply refusing to discuss economic issues. Reluctantly, and against the advice of Brotherhood representatives on the spot, the workers voted to strike on January 16, 1977. Reverend Bowie eloquently described to the House subcommittee what happened:

> During the past six months they have marched in the cold of night and the intense heat of the day as temperatures soared into the nineties. They have marched with such courage and dedication that the most hardened cynic would have to marvel at the human feeling to demonstrate their faith and belief in our system of law and justice. You see they have been told, and I have also told them, that, if they are right and if they follow the correct legal procedures, eventually the processes involved in the National Labor Relations Act would end in a just resolution of their problems.
>
> This confidence, however, has been most difficult in face of the physical and psychological abuse to which they have been subjected. Three strikers have been run over by cars leaving the plant, others have been intimidated by gun shots in the earthen bank near the highway where the strikers march by the company's guard. Nevertheless, the strikers have not retaliated in any violent form, because they believe that the NLRB and the courts will somehow offer them a just solution to their problems.

Police manhandle a striker at a mobile home manufacturing plant.

But how long must they wait? After six years, the company is still able to ignore, with apparent impunity, an election in which the overwhelming majority of employees voted in favor of representatives by the United Brotherhood of Carpenters.

As a remedy, organized labor turned to labor law reform. The White House had just broken faith on so-called situs-picketing. Under proposed legislation, construction unionists would have been able to make boycotts effective by being allowed to shut down entire job sites (as unions can in other industries), rather than picket one or two small, sub-contractor entrances at a construction site. "Situs picketing" had been barred by the Denver Building Site decision of the NLRB in 1951, and since upheld in the courts. The electrical work on a new building had been subcontracted to a non-union firm and the union men had walked off the job. The contractor

Brotherhood President William Sidell chairs AFL-CIO convention as President Jimmy Carter congratulates AFL-CIO President George Meany on his retirement.

filed charges with the NLRB, citing a Taft-Hartley provision which states: "It shall be an unfair labor practice for a labor organization . . . to engage in . . . a strike . . . where an object thereof is: . . . forcing or requiring . . . an employer or other person . . . to cease doing business with any other person. . . . ." Congress enacted a situs-picketing bill in the last days of 1975, which President Gerald Ford promised he would sign in the light of certain amendments that strengthened collective bargaining in the construction industry. However, President Ford vetoed the bill. Secretary of Labor John T. Dunlop resigned in protest.

Whether or not the veto was politically motivated, it certainly lost the President worker votes in the 1976 election. The Brotherhood endorsed Jimmy Carter, a reversal of its no-endorsement stand of four years previous. The election of Carter and of a Congress friendly to labor augured well for labor-law reform. Early in 1978, the Brotherhood secured protection against loss of earnings in the Redwood Extension Bill, which added 48,000 acres to the northern California Redwood National Park. Several millions of dollars was paid to lumber and sawmill workers for retraining made necessary by the loss of jobs. It was yet another indication that Congress was open to labor's needs.

The Labor Law Reform bill was drafted to eliminate the kinds of abuses cited by Ethel Johnson, Roger Taft, Pauline Frazier, and Reverend Bowie. It passed the House in October, 1977, and came before the Senate for debate on May 15. The Brotherhood's headquarters became a labor-law reform task force command center. Unions mounted a "Victims' Vigil" of workers unable to obtain justice under the present law. The victims met with AFL-CIO staffers and volunteers in devising strategy to defeat the filibuster in the Senate against labor reform. Despite their gallant efforts, labor-law reform failed by just two votes to achieve the two-thirds vote needed to end filibuster. In the following year, Carpenters played a key role in forestalling the repeal of the Davis-Bacon Act.

Institutions require an able as well as an innovative leadership to cope with the challenges of a complex and rapidly changing society. To maintain the quality of such leadership over generations is no easy task. The Brotherhood has evolved an orderly transition of leaders that has assured a continuity of well-trained officers.

When a General President retires, for example, the First Vice President moves up. By the time he became President in 1980, William Konyha brought to the position several decades of experience as a staff member and elected officer. A third-generation carpenter, Konyha learned the craft at age 14 working with his father, a Cleveland home builder. At the depths of the Depression, in 1932, be became an apprentice in Local Union 1180. Four years later, he became an organizer, signing up members in the lumberyards, mills and shops in the Cleveland area. During the war, he joined the Seabees, serving as a First Class Carpenter in the South Pacific.

After the war, Konyha was elected president of his local union. As the safety representative of the Cleveland District Council, he won widespread praise and many honors for his contributions to construction safety. As president of the Ohio State Council of Ohio from 1962 to 1972, he helped to establish state-wide programs for pensions, health and welfare benefits. He was elected General Executive Board member in 1970 and became Second Vice President in 1974 when he succeeded Herbert C. Skinner who died.

Each general officer and each member of the executive board undergoes a roughly analagous experience as they move up from apprentice to journeyman to elected union official. Yet, each brings to his post differences—in hometowns, education, temperament, to mention only a few—that enlarge the capabilities of the overall leadership of the union.

First General Vice President Patrick Campbell, as an instance, has 35 years of experience behind him as a union activist and officer. Shortly after his appointment in 1957 as an international representative, he was assigned to the Niagara Power Project, one of the largest construction jobs in the world, where he gained invaluable insight into giant construction as chairman of the labor-management committee for the entire operation.

Charles E. Nichols, a California resident, organized carpenters and other craftsmen in Hawaii and Alaska before being assigned to Northern California, Nevada, and Utah, where he broadened his background as chairman of the National Highway Committee for the latter two states. Of the present general officers, he has served the longest, having been named general treasurer in 1971.

Responsive and seasoned leadership works on the problems confronting the union as its first century draws to a close. Left to right are: Sigurd Lucassen, Second General Vice President; Patrick J. Campbell, First General Vice President; William Konyha, General President; John S. Rogers, General Secretary; and Charles E. Nichols, General Treasurer.

The Future Belongs to the Prepared

Sigurd Lucassen, named second vice president in 1980, is the newest among the top five general officers. He brings to the post invaluable experience as an employee trustee of the New Jersey Carpenters Welfare, Pension and Apprentice Funds as well as a range of union positions held in that state and along the East Coast.

General Secretary John S. Rogers, the youngest officer, was active in political affairs and ran for the New York State Assembly in 1960. A member of Local 1837, Babylon, N.Y., he participated in the Harvard University Trade Union Program. He serviced local unions in New England and New York as an international representative before becoming an assistant to the General President in 1969, a member of the General Executive Board in 1974, and General Secretary four years later.

The system evolved by the Brotherhood makes for a seasoned and responsive leadership. The test, of course, is in performance. The Brotherhood ended its one hundredth year some 820,000 members strong, organized in 2,083 local unions scattered throughout the United States and Canada. Scarcely a handful of highly-skilled craftsmen came together in 1881 to build a union. Over the years, they and their successors extended the bounds of their craft, adapted to a rapidly changing technology, reached out to organize millmen and other factory workers engaged in wood and related products manufacture, creating as they did so a modern trade union encompassing both craft and industrial workers. Their achievement became a model for others and is embodied in today's labor movement.

"The job of the next one hundred years," William Konyha has said, "is the unfinished work of the first one hundred years." Organizing the unorganized, educating union members and their families, creating a public opinion that will enable free trade unions to flourish—these are among the great challenges that lie ahead. Economic growth, equal opportunity, progress and social justice remain goals worth striving for. "What mighty portent is in the labor movement!" P. J. McGuire once wrote. "With hands and hearts together, with united funds and united interests, to stand for one another, day after day, year in and year out, in good times and in bad, who dare say what can they not accomplish? In the workshop and on the forum, at the ballot box and in every field of endeavor, they can right every wrong, and eradicate every evil oppressive to working people." The Carpenters today are well equipped to carry that struggle forward.

Each union develops a character comprised of the many elements that go into its make-up. Today, the members of the Brotherhood possess an astonishing array of crafts and skills. They work in a variety of industries and under widely differing circumstances. They may be found deep in the Canadian northwoods, at sawmills in northwest, beneath the murky waters of our harbours, in plants manufacturing trim or pre-fabricated modular housing, on oil rigs, in nuclear power plants, building helicopters in California, and installing astro-turf in giant sports stadiums. Peatmoss gatherers in the Maritime Provinces of Canada, musical instrument makers in the Middle West, manufacturers of fiberglass canopies and fiberglass boats, producers of portable toilets in Ohio, toilet seats in Mississippi, manufacturers of fiberglass hockey walls in Indiana, pet food workers in Missouri—all these and more are members of the Brotherhood. Each contributes something of value to the character of the Brotherhood.

Yet, certain traits are stronger because they are rooted in the origins of the union, in its traditions, in its central craft or industry. Novelist Edna Ferber once wrote, "I never have known a genuine carpenter who was not prideful in his work; gentle, forthright and humane in his nature. Carpenters are mysteriously likely to be men of intelligence and ingegrity; they are at once visionary and realistic." She thought it likely that these virtues had something to do with working with wood. "It just could be that the still living tonic of the long-felled trees clears the workman's brain and steadies his nerves and makes his hand sure and deft."

One could not claim all these virtues for all carpenters. Surely the novelist's acquaintances among craftsmen was limited. Carpenters, too, share the frailties of mankind. Yet, something of these qualities infused those who made P. J. McGuire's vision of brotherhood a reality and still infuses those builders of the twentieth century who so proudly belong to the United Brotherhood of Carpenters and Joiners of America, AFL-CIO-CLC.

ACKNOWLEDGMENTS

I want to thank the members and officers of the United Brotherhood of Carpenters and Joiners of America, AFL-CIO-CLC, for making this book possible. A great number of people contributed directly and indirectly to my growth in knowledge about the union and I wish I could list them all. I am grateful for their willingness to inform me about the Brotherhood and its past. I am, however, solely responsible for this work.

In particular, I would like to thank: John T. Dunlop, who introduced me to the union and offered wise counsel; to Walter Galenson, whose careful reading of the manuscript saved me from egregious error; to William Konyha, who opened the way and offered generous encouragement; to John S. Rogers, a fellow history buff, who provided insights that deepened my understanding; to Peter Terzick, whose perceptiveness proved enlightening; to Roger A. Sheldon, who gave sound advice; to Mary Zon, who found the right pictures; to Knox Burger, my agent, who arranged for publication; to Hubert Bermont, whose painstaking editorial guidance was so helpful; and to my wife, Harriet, as ever, patient.

BIBLIOGRAPHY

In writing this book I have drawn on materials in the ample archives of the United Brotherhood of Carpenters and Joiners of America, AFL-CIO, in Washington, D.C. The monthly issues of *The Carpenter*, convention proceedings and the correspondence of those involved in the union's affairs were invaluable. For general labor background and other details, I found the following useful:

Christie, Robert A. *Empire in Wood.* Ithaca, New York: Cornell University, 1956.

Commons, John R., and others. *History of Labour in the United States.* 2 vols. New York: The Macmillan Company, 1918.

Gompers, Samuel. *Seventy Years of Life and Labour.* New York: Agustus M. Kelley, Publishers, 1967.

Lieberman, Elias. *Unions Before the Bar.* New York: Oxford Book Company, 1960.

Lyon, David Bicholas. *The World of P. J. McGuire: A Study of the American Labor Movement.* Phd. dissertation, University of Minnesota, 1972.

Raddock, Maxwell C. *Portrait of an American Labor Leader: William L. Hutcheson.* New York: American Institute of Social Science, Inc., 1955.

Taft, Philip. *The A. F. of L. in the Time of Gompers.* New York: Harper & Brothers, 1957.

———. *The A. F. of L. from the Death of Gompers to the Merger.* New York: Harper & Brothers, 1959.

Seidman, Joel. *American Labor from Defense to Reconstruction.* Chicago:
The University of Chicago Press, 1953.
Whitney, Nathaniel Ruggles. *Jurisdiction in American Building-Trades
Union.* Baltimore: The Johns Hopkins Press, 1914.
Wolman, Leo. *The Boycott in American Trade Unions.* Baltimore: The
Johns Hopkins Press, 1916.

Thomas R. Brooks is the author of Toil and Trouble: A History of American Labor, which the New York Times Book Review called "A brilliant and original history of the American labor movement." A free-lance writer, Mr. Brooks has contributed articles on labor, politics and a variety of other subjects to periodicals such as *Commentary, New York Times Sunday Magazine, New York* and *The Reader's Digest.* He has been a farm hand, a soldier, a factory worker, union organizer, and labor editor.

INDEX

231